The Irresistible Bead

DESIGNING & CREATING
EXQUISITE BEADWORK JEWELRY

The Irresistible Bead

DESIGNING & CREATING EXQUISITE BEADWORK JEWELRY

· LINDA FRY KENZLE ·

kp krause publications
since 1952

Photography: Nick Novelli

Additional photography credits:

Don Carlo: Pages 2, 86, 93, 113
Jess Shirley: Page 92
Tom Van Eynde: Page 91
By bead artist: Pages 85, 89, 90
Handmade backgrounds: Don Carlo

Illustrations: Larry Meyer
Book design: Anthony Jacobson

Manufactured in the United States of America

Library of Congress Cataloging-in-Publication Data

Kenzle, Linda Fry.
    The irresistible bead : designing and creating exquisite beadwork
jewelry / Linda Fry Kenzle.
        p.   cm.
    Includes bibliographical references and index.
    ISBN 0-8019-8843-8
    1. Beadwork.   2. Jewelry making.   I. Title.
TT860.K46   1996
745.58′2—dc20   96-31937
                                                          CIP

1 2 3 4 5 6 7 8 9 0   7 8 9 0 1 2 3 4 5 6

To

Don Carlo,

with love,

"Barefoot Beaded Darling"

Contents

Chapter 4

BEADING ON A GROUND   48

Chapter 5

WOVEN BEADWORK   58

Chapter 6

POLYMER CLAY   72

BEADWORK GALLERY   84

Appendixes

ACKNOWLEDGMENTS

Writing a book is a huge undertaking that includes many people besides the author. I have the following people to thank for their part in creating this book:

My loving sweethearts: Don Carlo, Joshua, and Jeremiah

My great beading friends: Lily, Jean, Sue, and Dawn

My superb photographer: Nick Novelli

My excellent illustrator: Larry Meyer

My sensational editors: Mary Green, Susan Keller, and Linda Biemiller

Everyone else at Chilton: Bruce, Sandy, Tony, Nancy, and the others who make a book come together so smoothly

My gracious bead artists: Ariel Brandt, Sandy Forrington, Bette M. Kelley, Catherine Lippert, Nome May, NanC Meinhardt, Regine, Miriam Salzer, and Justine West

My ingenious bead hunters: Carol Young and Viki Konopasek

All of the generous librarians at the Fox River Grove Library

And the indispensable others: Alice Scherer of The Center for the Study of Beadwork; Holnam, Inc.; Loew-Cornell, Inc.; June Taylor, Inc.; and anyone else who shared their expertise that I may have forgotten to list…thank you.

INTRODUCTION

According to archeologists, beads have been in existence for 20,000 years. Small stone cones that were shaped by being ground on rocks have been found in archeological digs. The cones are identified as beads because each one has a hole purposely pierced into its top.

It is easy to imagine how these ancient beads were used for personal adornment, because people are still adorning their bodies with beads (probably in much the same way) after all these years. We love self-expression—it echoes from our ancient selves to our modern existence—and we simply adore beads.

The enchantment with beads often starts with one irresistible bead, a bead that attracts your attention, practically calling to you. You want to possess that bead's magic, to own the bead and to wear it.

Beadwork itself is a soothing, seductive process, a process of one bead, then another, rhythmically proceeding forward, compelled by the beader's urge to see the finished piece. It is a thrill to see what a pile of beads and thread—worked by your own hands—can become.

Beading is also an exciting process. I hope you enjoy the collection I have designed for you. Perhaps they will tickle you into exploring a new technique you may have hesitated to try before. I have placed key jewelry making techniques that you will use over and over again in special boxes called At-a-Glance. You won't have to search through projects to find out how to add a clasp, add a knot cover, create beaded coil edging, and so on—the information is right at your fingertips whenever you need it.

This book covers a wide range of techniques and styles, ranging from techniques derived from the exquisite beadwork of Native Americans to techniques whose roots go back to beading done in Russia, Europe, and ancient Egypt. Chapter 1 is dedicated to an in-depth discussion of the elements of design, providing structure and artistic guidance as you explore the projects and techniques presented in the rest of the book.

In Chapter 2, which features basic wirework, you'll find elegant earrings, a smart brooch, and stickpins, as well as the uptown, easy-to-make Cleopatra Necklace. Also included in this chapter is the Rock Wrap Bracelet, a lovely piece that is modern in design yet ancient in mood.

Chapter 3 focuses on bead stringing, presenting a group of popular close-to-the-neck necklaces, as well as the sensational-looking Beaded Skeleton Watch. Phoenix Rising, done in fringe work, is a stunning heirloom-type piece with a Native American edge.

Beading on fabric and leather is the subject of Chapter 4. This chapter offers a pin made from a beautiful cabochon caressed by seed beads, a contemporary geometric pin, and an eye-catching piece called Flight of Fantasy, which features a beaded bird accented with beaded feathers.

Chapter 5, which introduces woven beadwork, takes you on a journey through Comanche and peyote stitch. The projects in this chapter include an ageless pair of diamond-shaped earrings, a 1950s-style flower necklace, a sleek modern bracelet, and the exquisite Night Sky Peyote Pouch.

The last chapter explores the basics of polymer clay. It begins with a basic necklace made from handmade beads, then challenges you with a piece made of gilded beads and finally, an artistic sculptural necklace called Sapphire and Sunshine.

Those of you interested in creating your own exclusive designs may wish to spend some time in Chapter 1 learning about the fundamentals of design. In addition, each chapter is followed by a special illustrated section called Designer's Notebook, which may further tempt you into exploring the possibilities of beadwork design. You'll also find specific design charts in Appendix F that will be useful for designing your own jewelry, regardless which of the techniques—wirework, bead stringing, beading on a ground, daisy stitch, brick stitch, peyote stitch, or polymer clay—you select.

The end of the book offers up a wonderful gallery of beadwork by artists from all over the country. It is a veritable feast for the eyes! Perhaps these pieces will lend you inspiration as well.

I have also included appendixes and other resources to give you easy access to important information you'll need as you bead. The appendixes include Bead Sizes, Jewelry Findings, Precious and Semiprecious Stones, and Birthstones. In addition, there is a Beader's Glossary (make good use of this if I use terms you aren't familiar with), a section of Recommended Reading, and a list of Resources.

I hope you'll use this book as a jumping-off point to design and produce beautiful pieces of beadwork jewelry. I'd love to see your creations. Send photos or slides to me at P.O. Box 177, Fox River Grove, IL 60021, for possible inclusion in a future book.

L.F.K.

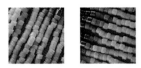

"It is well-known that snowflakes, though following basic patterns, are never exactly alike. Neither is any seashell exactly like any other seashell, nor any tongue of flame, nor any ocean wave, nor cloud alike. The artist who would create truly original designs must learn to see the individuality of his inspirations and to respect it. He must train his eye to look beneath the general shape of things to the variation that create interest. *For the creative artist, individuality is the most important design characteristic of all.*

It has been said that nothing new is ever created in the world of matter. The truth carries over to design. Every design is based on age-old forms whether they are found in nature or simple geometric lines and figures in an abstract way. Yet a new approach is like a spring bubbling out of a hillside; the water is the same as the water that has been used and drunk for centuries, yet it is always new, always fresh, always satisfying because it comes forth in its own way, in its own place...."

Marjorie Elliott Bevlin
Design Through Discovery

CHAPTER 1
DESIGNING YOUR OWN JEWELRY

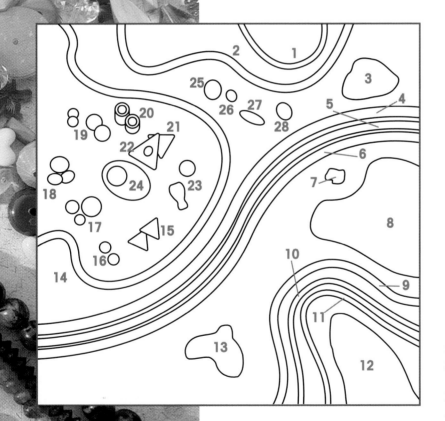

1. Labradorite tubes
2. Hematite stars
3. Unakite
4. Blue crystals
5. Antique faceted beads
6. Rose quartz interspersed with hematite
7. Gold-plated beads
8. German Plexiglas
9. Picasso jasper
10. Antique black beads
11. Labradorite rounds
12. German Plexiglas
13. German Plexiglas
14. Coral (stem)
15. Blue lace agate
16. Polymer clay beads
17. African hammered brass
18. Bali silver
19. Fluted brass
20. Olive glass
21. Don-don Hawaiian wedding bead
22. Howlite
23. India glass
24. Rose quartz donut
25. Transfer bead
26. Venetian glass
27. India glass
28. Scarab

Beautiful beadwork jewelry is beautiful because of good design. Good design is accomplished by employing the basic elements of design that are used in all artwork, from fine paintings to exquisite jewelry. Line, shape, texture, and color—the elements of design—can be used in a deliberate way to make your work exciting and powerful. Design elements can be employed intentionally to evoke a particular mood, and a change in a single element can transform a piece from calm to explosive. When you design your own pieces, what springs forth will come from your life experiences, making your beadwork a powerful expression of self.

Let's take a look at each of the elements of design individually to explore the possibilities.

LINE

A horizontal line is calming. Think of a field landscape...very calm and soothing. A horizontal line lends a meditative quality to a finished piece (see the Jeweled Diamond Earrings on page 61). When the line begins to become animated and curved, it adds action to a piece. A soft rolling line shows some movement and energy, as in the Starburst Necklace on page 32. As the line becomes exaggerated in size, forming a larger loop, the movement intensifies and thus creates more activity in a piece (see the Sapphire and Sunshine Neckpiece on page 78). And, when the loops sharpen into points, the results are dramatic

Born to Be a Butterfly
by Justine West
This piece balances many curvilinear lines with a bit of tension produced by the strong verticals created by the butterfly's body. It also has good shape and good texture (note the raised beads in the middle). The color is bright (mostly primaries), giving a freshness to the newly transformed butterfly image. This piece is made from various sizes of seed beads, bugles, and Czechoslovakian glass, worked in card beading technique.

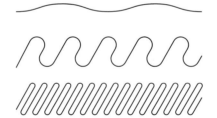

Figure 1.1

and very expressive, as seen in the Contempo Triangle Pin on page 51.

If we go back and take the straight horizontal line and tilt it on an angle we create diagonal lines. A diagonal always represents activity and movement. Think of a sky full of diagonal clouds: it is active and changing. As the diagonal moves from the horizon on an upward tilt it becomes more energized (Figure 1.2). Again, the Contempo Triangle Pin (page 51) provides a good example of this design quality.

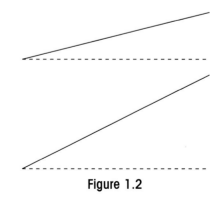

Figure 1.2

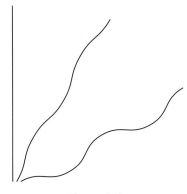

Figure 1.3

A vertical line reaches toward the heavens and thus symbolizes growth and spirituality. A straight vertical has a calm quality just like a straight horizontal line does. When the line begins to bend it attains movement, and the more exaggerated the curves, the more active the line (Figure 1.3). In fact, when any line becomes curvy and freeform it denotes intense activity. Think of the movement of a dancer. As a person goes from a standing position to performing the movements of a ballet, the body comes alive; the arms move away from the body, and the legs become moving angular projections. In a similar fashion, see how the projections—the beaded loop adornment—add movement to the stickpin on page 17?

You can use the element of line to design an entire piece of jewelry to reflect whatever statement you wish to make. Also consider line when choosing individual beads for a project. For example, a solid-colored bead will make a piece more restive than will a multicolored bead done in a swirly pattern like that of Picasso jasper.

SHAPE

A square is the classic quiet shape. Even if you only see a part of it your mind completes the square shape, giving it bulk and weightiness. Squares give an earthy quality to a design.

Rectangles—elongated squares—are less weighty than true squares. They are seen as receptacles. Bags (like the Night Sky Peyote pouch on page 65) and boxes are most often rectangular.

The circle is more lively than the square or rectangle. You know that if a circle could somehow be released from the design it would roll like a child's ball. A circle is playful—even comical—and can be used to soften a design (for example, note how the amber bead atop the Venetian Ice Brooch on page 15 softens the large rectangular bead).

If you take the square and place it on point you get a diamond shape. The diamond is more active (see those sharp diagonal lines?) than the sedate square and offers a feeling of

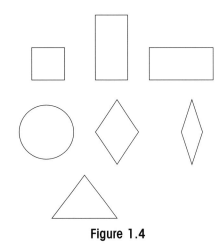

Figure 1.4

excitement (that's why a harlequin's costume is composed of diamonds). The more pointed a diamond becomes the more activity it conveys. Use diamond shapes in your jewelry design when you want to express action.

Cut a diamond in half and you have a triangle. A triangle is the strongest shape known to man (think of the pyramids, for example, or the classic triangular roof). The triangle also has cosmic connotations: man, heaven, and earth; the Holy Trinity; earth, wind, and fire; and so on. Because of its diagonal lines and sharp points, a triangle is an active form. The Lucky Pennies Necklace on page 34 shows how this form can be used creatively in jewelry design.

TEXTURE

Smooth beads are suave and sophisticated. Shiny beads, which reflect more light than other beads, also create a sleek look and tend to attract attention when a piece is being worn (the child in us is always attracted to a shiny bauble!).

Textured beads, like rose-cut garnets and dotted polymer clay, bring interest to a piece and make the viewer want to take a closer look. Another way to use texture in a piece to create visual interest is to take the beads off of a flat plane and work them texturally. A good example of this approach is seed bead branches, that is, seed beads strung to project out like the branches of a tree. Fringe also

Note that warm colors protrude whereas cool colors recede.

To help you visualize these color concepts, let's take a look at some examples from the projects in this book. Phoenix Rising (page 39) is worked in cool colors. The Contempo Triangle Pin (page 51) uses hot reds and yellows, tempered by a dash of black. The Sapphire and Sunshine Neckpiece (page 78) uses both hot and cold colors to balance the design.

NEUTRALS

Black, white, brown, gray, and clear can be used to accent or define any of the other colors. All are readily available in seed beads and Delicas.

Many semiprecious beads fall into the neutral category. Hematite and onyx are classic shiny black. Howlite is a good white even though it is lightly streaked with gray—from a distance the eye reads the stone as pure white. Pearls and white quartz are other good whites.

Browns include picture jasper and the shiny tigereye. Black-and-white snowflake obsidian reads gray, as does smoky labradorite. Totally clear beads are plain glass; crystals are sparkly clear beads.

METALLICS

Gold, silver, copper, and brass beads add sparkle to a piece. You can select precious metals—14 karat gold and sterling silver—if price is no object. Otherwise, plated and painted beads are readily available. Note that plat-

Texture #6
by Ariel Brandt
This beautiful piece uses a variety of beads—smooth, fluted, incised, amorphous—and various shapes and sizes to create exciting texture. (Materials used in this piece: seed beads, India glass, bugles, nacre, Venetian glass, olive glass, metal beads, and Delicas, with a goldtone clasp.)

creates visual interest and movement and thus attracts the eye.

COLOR
SINGULAR COLOR

Color is the most determinate factor in creating a mood within a piece. Each color by itself is associated with a feeling or with several feelings, and each color also connotes a temperature. Here are the ways colors are perceived in the United States:

BLUE (cool) serenity and peacefulness

GREEN (cool) money and jealousy; also associated with ecology

PURPLE (cool) royalty; also eccentricity

RED (warm) blood, war; passion, love

YELLOW (warm) playful; warning

ORANGE (warm) naivete; intensity; activates the salivary glands

As the color darkens the temperature becomes intensified, cool to cold, warm to hot. When the color is lightened the temperature lessens. For example when red is lightened to pink it loses its heat (passion) and cools to become soft and innocent.

Color Wheel

Outside ring, clockwise from center top: red seed beads, 11/0; red-violet seed beads, 16/0; violet German Plexiglas; blue-violet Japanese Delicas; blue lapis lazuli chips; blue-green amazonite, 10mm round; green malachite, 4mm round; yellow-green ceramic bead; yellow citrine tubes; yellow-orange transparent lined beads, 11/0; orange German Plexiglas; red-orange carnelian chips. *Inside ring, clockwise from upper right:* translucent white glass; clear glass rondels with white stripe; pearl; gold and silver seeds; silver-lined rondel; three ivory beads and three pearl seed beads. *Center:* crystals.

ing wears off in time, so you may wish to reserve plated beads for fun pieces that don't take a great deal of time to construct. One bead shop owner has suggested spraying metallic beads with clear acrylic spray before using them.

There currently isn't any research indicating whether the spray helps retard the flaking of the plating, but you might want to conduct your own experiments.

Another option is to select glass beads like those from India and Italy that have gold fused inside the glass (for example, see the large bead in the Venetian Ice Brooch on page 15). They will remain pristine forever and their price isn't as high as that of solid beads of 14 karat gold.

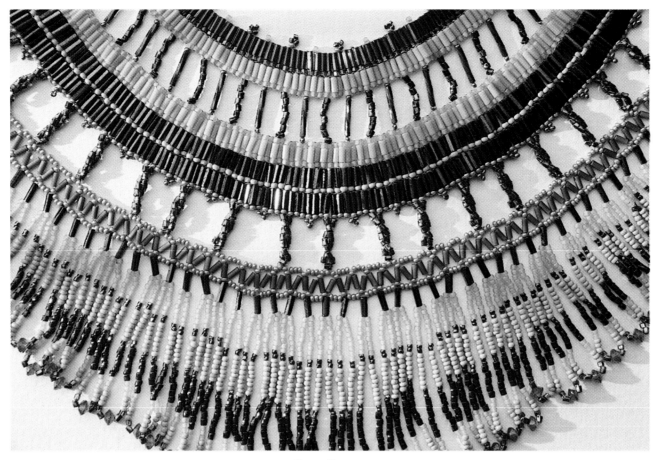

Bryce Canyon
by Bette M. Kelley
Bette is an amazing colorist. In this piece she interpreted the colors of the beautiful landscapes out West. If you've been there this piece will instantly transport you back. Notice how unusual the seed bead and bugle color combinations are and how well they work together.

Metallics are eye-catching and add a great deal of visual excitement to a piece. To see an example of this, look at the Simple Elegance Earrings on page 13, which use large gold fluted beads as stunning accents.

COMBINING COLORS

On the bead color wheel on page 5 you can see that the primaries—red, yellow, and blue—form a triangle within the wheel. The primaries in their pure form are considered basic and naive. All colors are created from these three colors. On the color wheel the secondary colors—orange, green, and violet—form another triangle. Each secondary color is created by combining two primaries. Equal parts of yellow and red make orange, while green is a combination of yellow and blue, and violet is a combination of red and blue. (If you have never played with paint and you find the color wheel to be merely an abstract intellectual concept I invite you to experience the magic. Buy a tube of each primary and a paint brush and dig in! The results will amaze you.)

Next we move to the tertiaries. Each of these colors is a combination of a primary and a secondary color. By their names alone you will be able to recognize the obvious combinations: for example, blue mixed with violet makes blue-violet. The other tertiaries are red-violet, red-orange, yellow-orange, yellow-green, and blue-green. You may know these colors by their colloquial names: purple, fuchsia, tangerine, coral, chartreuse, and turquoise.

Any color lightened with white is called a tint. Pink, for example, is a tint of red. A shade is made by adding black to a color.

From the basic color wheel we can move on to the traditional color schemes:

MONOCHROMATIC This color scheme uses many shades and tints of a single color; for example: light blue, medium blue, and navy blue.

COMPLEMENTARY This scheme uses colors directly across from each other on the color wheel. Red and green are complementary colors. When complementary colors of equal intensity are used together they create a flashing effect. If that is the effect you desire, that's fine; otherwise, just use a tint or shade of one of the complements so the colors won't "shimmy."

SPLIT COMPLEMENT To use this color scheme, select one color (green, for instance), draw an imaginary line from it across the color wheel to find its complement (red), and use the colors found on either side of the complement (in this case, red-orange and red-violet). Thus, one possible split complementary color scheme would be green, coral, and fuchsia.

ANALOGOUS In this color scheme, colors that lie next to each other are used together; for instance,

Crystal Cave
by Linda Fry Kenzle
Another way to use a monochromatic scheme effectively is to use pattern-on-pattern. In this piece the body of the bag combines three different blacks—a matte black, shiny black, and an iridescent black. Pattern-on-pattern creates a subtle, sophisticated look. (The beads used in this piece are Delicas and Swarovski crystals.)

blue, blue-green, and green, or yellow-orange, yellow, and yellow-green.

What I have discussed so far is the traditional way to use color. Now I would like to share with you a most interesting method I call the affinity of color.

LINDA'S AFFINITY OF COLOR

This unique color theory is based on the B-Bright, L-Light, D-Dark concept. The idea is to use brights, lights, and darks to create an exciting color scheme. The *relationship* of the colors, not the actual hue, is of primary importance. The only rule in the B-L-D concept is to use the colors in unequal amounts. Usually the Bright is used as a "spark," so it is used in the least amount. For example, white (Bright), yellow (Light), and red (Dark) would be one possibility. Here are three sample color schemes to show how a single color (in this case medium blue) can be the B, the L, or the D of a particular scheme:

BRIGHT	LIGHT	DARK
1. medium blue	celadon	chocolate
2. yellow	medium blue	burgundy
3. white	pink	medium blue

You can also use as many colors as you chose, as long as you remember to use the Brights, Lights, and Darks in unequal amounts. Here's one possibility:

BRIGHTS	LIGHTS	DARKS
silver	orange	purple
pale gray	dusty blue	black
	cinnamon	dark gray
	melon	

Rewired Circuitry
by Linda Fry Kenzle
Here's a good example of the "affinity of color" design system. In this piece, the Bright is the turquoise, the Light is the yellow, and the Dark is the purple. Notice also how the solid rectangular shape is broken up with a soft line to add action. The fringe adds a kinetic accent and a lot of interesting texture. (In this piece, Delicas, seed beads, and glass beads are done in peyote stitch.)

The stickpin on page 17 shows a simple B-L-D grouping. In this piece, the turquoise and gold beads are the Brights, the crystals are the Light, and the black beads are the obvious Dark.

The best way to grasp the concept of affinity of color is to analyze paintings by the masters. Pick out the Brights, Lights, and Darks and note how they are used in unequal amounts. See how wonderfully this concept works? Try it out on one of your pieces. I think you'll love it!

BASIC JEWELRY DESIGN

CREATING A FOCAL POINT

A focal point is an element that draws the eye, such as a large bead surrounded by smaller beads in a pendant, pin, or bracelet (see Figure 1.5). A focal point bead is usually quite large in relation to the other beads, and although it usually falls in the center of a piece, it may be located off-center to create a deliberately asymmetrical look. (See the Triple Pendant Necklace on page 27 for an example of focal point.)

All other beads used in conjunction with the focal point bead are called secondary beads. Secondary beads usually pick up some of the colors found in the focal point bead, but they may instead be complementary in color. Although all of the beads can be the same, it is quite fashionable to mix up the beads by

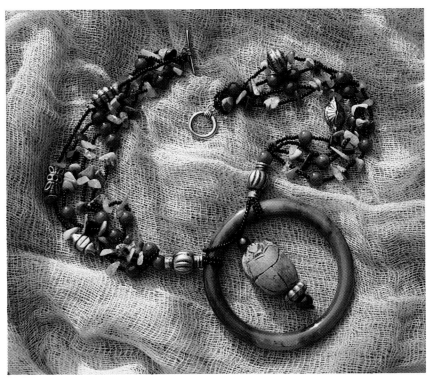

Texture #27
by Ariel Brandt
Look at the strong focal point in this piece. Beautiful jade combines with an Egyptian scarab, seed beads, fancy metal beads, and semiprecious stone chips to make this a nice cross-cultural piece.

METALS

Metallic beads can be interspersed in a design to offer shine and diversion. Traditionally, the metal is matched to the bead color: for example, gray beads are accented with silver beads, and brown beads are accented with gold beads. Many colors (such as blue, red, and green) can be dressed up with either silver or gold. Brass is an excellent accent to African trade beads. Lately I've become enchanted by copper beads and am using them extensively in my work; I like copper with almost any color bead. In my earlier work I was thrilled with the two-tone look of combining gold and silver beads in one piece. Remember, you are the designer, so use the metallics as you prefer, making your own statement.

FINDINGS

Most jewelry findings—clasps, French hooks, jump rings, etc.— come in silvertone and goldtone and also in the precious metals. (See Appendix C at the back of this book.) The new iridescent novelty metal called niobium comes in exciting colors like old gold, turquoise, and purple, and you can match the color of the finding to the beads you are using. With the niobium the finding may even be the starting point of a design, with the beads being selected to match or coordinate with the finding.

If you are unable to find a clasp to match a beaded piece you can create a self-made toggle by continuing the length of

Figure 1.5

size and color to add variety. In general, an eclectic mix of beads creates a more pleasing design. If you are not using a defined focal point to create visual balance, employ the sensual quality of rhythm. Rhythm occurs with any repeats in a design. For example, a necklace might call for a pattern of three 4mm pink quartz beads and one black hematite seed bead to be repeated for the desired length of the piece. Any repeats—whether of size, color, line, or shape—produce a rhythm, and hence a feeling of natural balance.

strung beads and fashioning a self-loop. Finish the other side of the necklace with a toggle stick. Complete instructions for creating a toggle clasp can be found in my previous book, *Dazzle: Creating Artistic Jewelry and Distinctive Accessories* (Chilton, 1995).

Before you proceed with the techniques and projects in the remaining chapters, please spend a few minutes getting acquainted with the Appendixes and other resources at the back of this book if you haven't already done so. They are included to provide quick help as you journey through the world of beading. Now let's get started playing with those beautiful beads!

BASIC JEWELRY MAKING TOOLS AND SUPPLIES

TOOLS

Jewelry pliers (those designed especially for jewelry making are the best all-around pliers)

Snipe-nose pliers

Round-nose pliers

Flat-nose pliers

Wire cutters

Embroidery scissors

NEEDLES

#12 sharps (these are my favorite needles; they have a very slim shaft and will go through the tiniest beads, yet the hole will accommodate Nymo and cotton-covered polyester thread)

Beading needles (available in a long length for loom work and a shorter length for bead stringing, beading on a ground, etc.)

Wire needle (the large eye is easy to thread and collapses while beading)

Beeswax (used to coat any threads to decrease tangling; not necessary on coated threads)

Needle threader (handy if you have trouble threading the tiny eyes on beading needles)

THREADS AND CORDS

You may use the thinner threads (silk, nylon, etc.) single or doubled. My own preference is to use a single strand of cotton-covered polyester. I have pieces of jewelry (both strung and woven) made with this type of thread 15 to 20 years ago that show no signs of thread deterioration.

I have used all of the following threads and cords for jewelry making. Try each to find what you like best.

Cotton-covered polyester quilting thread

Tigertail (can kink)

Nylon thread (use doubled for heavy pieces)

Waxed linen thread (great for large-holed beads)

Nymo thread (use doubled for heavy pieces)

Silk thread (use doubled for heavy pieces)

Kevlar (exceptionally strong)

GLUES AND ADHESIVES

E-6000 jewelry cement

BOND 527

Model airplane glue

Clear fingernail polish

CHAPTER 2
WIREWORK

Just a bit of wire and some striking beads can be turned into sleek, sophisticated pieces of jewelry. The chapter begins with Simple Elegance, a pair of earrings done on head pins, and Venetian Ice, an exquisite eye-pin brooch. Next, long stickpins are lavishly decorated with a cluster of unique beads. Later in the chapter the projects become slightly more complicated and elaborate. Cleopatra Necklace is a fancy, detailed piece ornamented with dangles made on head pins. Rock Wrap, the final piece in the chapter, is a slinky bracelet that features the wire-wrapping technique.

SIMPLE ELEGANCE EARRINGS

A few beautiful beads, two head pins, and a pair of French hook findings are all it takes to create a great-looking pair of earrings. If you don't have pierced ears, clasp-type earring findings will work just as well. Turn to the Designer's Notebook pages at the end of the chapter to see some similar earrings that may give you ideas for your own designs.

ℳATERIALS

2 head pins, 3" long

Gold metallic seed beads, size 11/0

Enough beads to fill the pins (I used antique glass beads, plus large fluted golden balls for accent)

2 French hook earring findings

𝒯OOLS AND SUPPLIES

Jewelry pliers

AT-A-GLANCE

ℱORMING ℒOOPS

1. Using the snipe-nose jewelry pliers, grab the head pin close to the last bead and bend it to form a right angle.

2. Now grab the end of the pin with the pliers. Turn the pliers to form the loop. *Note:* If you have trouble forming the loop in one motion, grab the end of the pin, turn it halfway, reposition the pliers, and then make one more turn to form the loop.

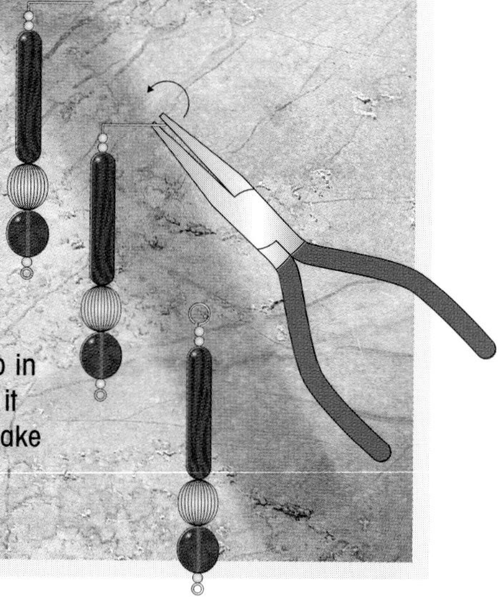

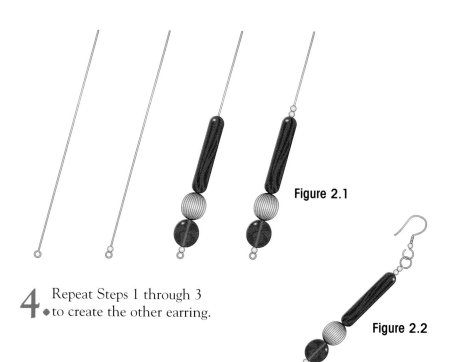

𝒯ECHNIQUE

1. Slip one gold seed bead on a head pin. Add other beads to within ¾″ of the end of the pin. Add two more gold seed beads. (See Figure 2.1.)

2. Follow the directions in the box to finish the end of the head pin by forming a loop.

3. Use pliers to open the loop at the bottom of the French hook finding. Slip the loop of the beaded head pin on the opened earring loop (Figure 2.2). Close the loop using the pliers.

4. Repeat Steps 1 through 3 to create the other earring.

Figure 2.1

Figure 2.2

VENETIAN ICE BROOCH

he elegant bead showcased in this piece is lined with gold foil. Just add flirty eye-pin dangles and an amber topknot for a gorgeous, go-with-everything brooch. For inspiring examples of similar brooches, see the Designer's Notebook pages at the end of the chapter.

MATERIALS

Venetian glass bead (the one I used is ½″ × 1″; use a bead of a similar size to maintain the proportion of the final piece)

4 gold eye pins, 2½″ long

3 aurora borealis bugle beads, 1½″ long

1 amber bead, 6mm

1 pin back, ¾″ long

TOOLS AND SUPPLIES

Jewelry pliers
Wire cutters
Jewelry cement

TECHNIQUE

1. Insert one eye pin through the large glass bead. Add the amber bead to the eye pin. Bend the eye pin to the back of the amber bead (Figure 2.3). Add a dab of jewelry cement to the tip of the eye pin and immediately insert it back into the large bead.

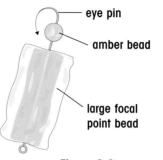

eye pin

amber bead

large focal point bead

Figure 2.3

2. Place one of the aurora borealis bugle beads on one of the remaining eye pins. Snip off ¼″ of the eye pin using the wire cutters. Follow the instructions in the box on page 14 to form the loops.

3. Repeat Step 2 to create the other two dangles.

4. Using pliers, bend open the formed loop of a dangle

Figure 2.4

and place the dangle on the loop at the bottom of the eye pin coming out of the large bead; close the loop (Figure 2.4).

5. Add on the other two dangles in the same manner; note that the dangles will hang better if the loops of the outside dangles face in one direction and the loop of the center dangle faces in the opposite direction (Figure 2.5).

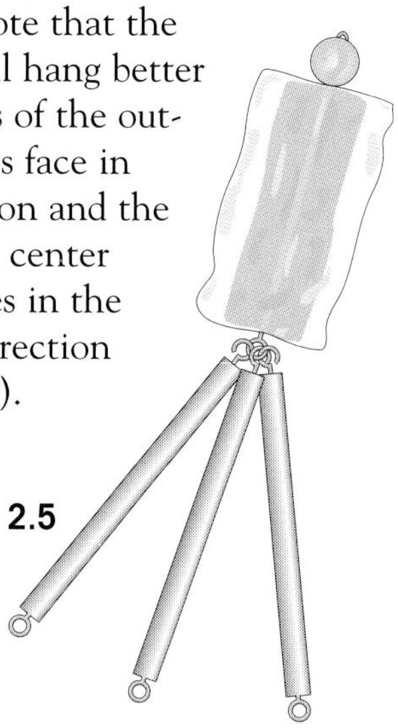

Figure 2.5

6. Glue the pin back lengthwise to the back of the large bead. Allow the adhesive to dry thoroughly.

FANCY STICKPINS

A stickpin is just a long length of silver or gold wire with a very sharp end—but add a collection of novel beads and you have a striking ornament. Stab a beaded stickpin into the side of your hat, or place one on the lapel of your favorite jacket for a nice effect. These are so easy you can make up a batch in an hour! For more stickpin ideas, see the Designer's Notebook pages at the end of the chapter.

MATERIAL

Stickpin (if you are using a lapel pin with a head, snip the head off before trying this project)

Beads

Crimps (optional)

TOOLS AND SUPPLIES

Jewelry cement

Crimp setter or jewelry pliers (optional)

Beading needle and thread (for bead ornament)

TECHNIQUE

1. Select beads by making trial arrangements on the pin. Once you have a design you are pleased with, remove the beads in order.

2. *To create the optional beaded loop adornment:* For each loop, string seed beads on a piece of thread to the length desired. Place the thread ends together. Place the needle on the thread ends and insert the needle through the bead that will be the topmost bead on the pin (Figure 2.6). Remove the needle, pulling it all the way through the top bead and allowing the threads to hang down.

Figure 2.6

3. Add the beads to the pin. You can glue all the beads in place on the pin, or you can place a crimp on first, add the beads, and then glue only the topmost bead in place.

Figure 2.7

4. *To finish a pin with the beaded loop adornment:* Add the beads to the pin using either of the two methods described in Step 3; then add glue to the end of the pin and place the topmost bead in place so the threads come out toward the sharp end (Figure 2.7). Cut off the thread ends. Allow the glue to dry.

CLEOPATRA NECKLACE

his piece is a modern version of the Egyptian broad collar necklaces. The dangles only appear on the front display area of the necklace. If you want something more elaborate, go ahead and attach beaded dangles around the entire length of the necklace. The colors for this piece came from the wonderful antique glass beads that have the look of watermelon tourmaline. To see illustrations of similar necklaces with different design features, turn to the Designer's Notebook pages at the end of the chapter.

MATERIALS

41 grass-green faceted
   beads, 10mm
2 pink beads, 8mm
2 coral beads, 8mm
6 coral beads, 6mm
6 pink beads, 4mm
24 antique glass tooth beads,
   4mm × 8mm
58 gold seed beads, size
   11/0
6 gold head pins, 3"
1 gold fancy clasp

TOOLS AND SUPPLIES

Jewelry pliers
Clear fingernail polish
Beading needle, #12
Thread

AT-A-GLANCE

ADDING A CLASP

1. Take the thread through the hole on the clasp as many times as possible. Tie a knot.

2. Place the needle on the thread end and insert the needle through 10 or so strung beads. Cut away any excess thread, trimming as close to the bead the thread exits as possible. Remove the needle.

3. Tie the jump ring on the other thread end. Knot, add a needle, and then insert the needle back through some of the strung beads. Cut away excess thread.

4. Dot the knots with clear fingernail polish.

TECHNIQUE

1. Place beads on each of the head pins using the following sequence: 1 gold seed, 1 green bead, 1 gold seed, 1 antique tooth bead, 1 gold seed, 1 small coral bead, 1 gold seed, 1 antique tooth bead, 1 gold seed, 1 green bead, 1 gold seed, 1 small pink bead.

2. Using the jewelry pliers, grab the end of the head pin and twist it into a loop (see instructions on page 14). Repeat for all dangles.

3. Cut a 24″ length of thread. Tie one end of the thread to one end of the clasp, following the directions in the box. Do not cut the short thread end. Add the needle to the other end of the thread.

4. String beads as follows: 1 gold seed, 1 antique tooth bead, 1 large pink bead, 7 green beads, * 1 gold seed, 1 antique tooth bead, 1 gold seed, 1 green bead; repeat from the * three more times. Now add 1 antique tooth bead, 1 gold seed, 1 large coral bead, 1 gold seed, ** 1 green bead, 1 dangle; repeat from the ** five more times. Work the other side of the necklace by repeating (in reverse) the sequence already strung. Remove the needle.

5. Tie the thread to the other end of the clasp. Place the needle on the thread ends and work them back into the strung beads on either side of the clasp. Seal the knots with a bit of clear fingernail polish.

ROCK WRAP BRACELET

Once you learn this wire-wrapping technique you can fashion any irregularly shaped rock into sleek jewelry. In this piece, green aventurine and clear quartz are wire-wrapped and then accented with carnelian column beads. The bracelet finishes at 8″ long. If you prefer a shorter length, just delete one wire-wrapped rock from each side. Other examples of Rock Wrap Bracelets are pictured in the Designer's Notebook section at the end of the chapter.

MATERIALS

1 spool 20 gauge silver wire

3 carnelian column beads,
    5mm × 20mm

2 clear quartz rocks, 1/2″ long

2 green aventurine rocks, 1/2″
    long

4 silver jump rings, 5mm

1 silver jump ring, 8mm

1 silver lobster claw clasp

TOOLS AND SUPPLIES

2 pairs of jewelry pliers, or a
    vise and a pair of jewelry
    pliers

TECHNIQUE

1. Cut a 6″ length of wire. Form the center of the wire into a loop. Place another length of wire into the loop. Put the wire in a vise or hold it with a pair of pliers. Form a cage with the four strands of wire (Figure 2.8). Insert the rock (Figure 2.9). Take the other pair of pliers and grasp the four wire ends so they hold the rock tightly. Twist the top wires so they fit snugly, conforming to the shape of the rock. Cut away three of the wire strands. Smooth the wire ends around the single wire strand (Figure 2.10). Cut off the excess wire and form the remaining length of wire into a loop (Figure 2.11)(see instructions on page 14).

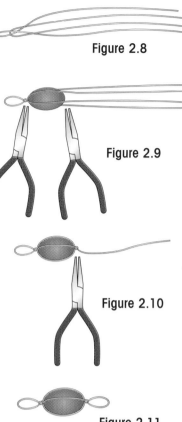

Figure 2.8

Figure 2.9

Figure 2.10

Figure 2.11

(see instructions on page 14).

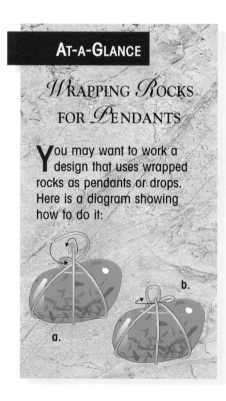

AT-A-GLANCE

Wrapping Rocks for Pendants

You may want to work a design that uses wrapped rocks as pendants or drops. Here is a diagram showing how to do it:

a.

b.

2. Cut three pieces of wire 2″ long. Center one of the carnelian column beads on each piece of wire. Using the jewelry pliers fashion the ends into loops (Figure 2.12).

Figure 2.12

3. To assemble the bracelet, attach one column bead to one clear wire-wrapped rock with a jump ring (see box). Then add another jump ring to the other end of the clear

AT-A-GLANCE

Attaching a Jump Ring

Don't distort a jump ring by opening it with a side-to-side motion. Instead, move one end to the front and one end to the back using one motion. Slide the jump ring in place, then close the ring by reversing the motion. The jump ring ends will then fit together perfectly.

wire-wrapped rock and attach the green wire-wrapped rock. Attach one more column bead (this is the center bead). (See Figure 2.13.)

4. Add the remaining beads in reverse order.

5. Attach the large jump ring to one end of the bracelet. Attach a jump ring and the lobster claw clasp to the other end of the bracelet.

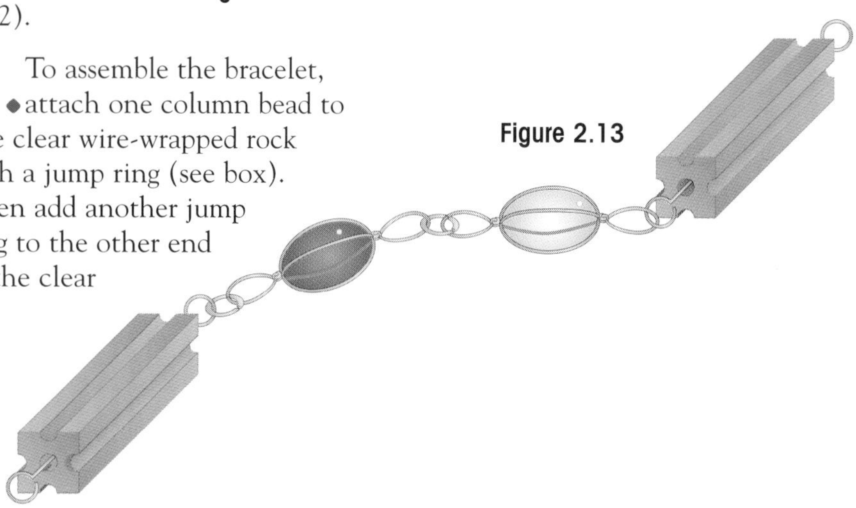

Figure 2.13

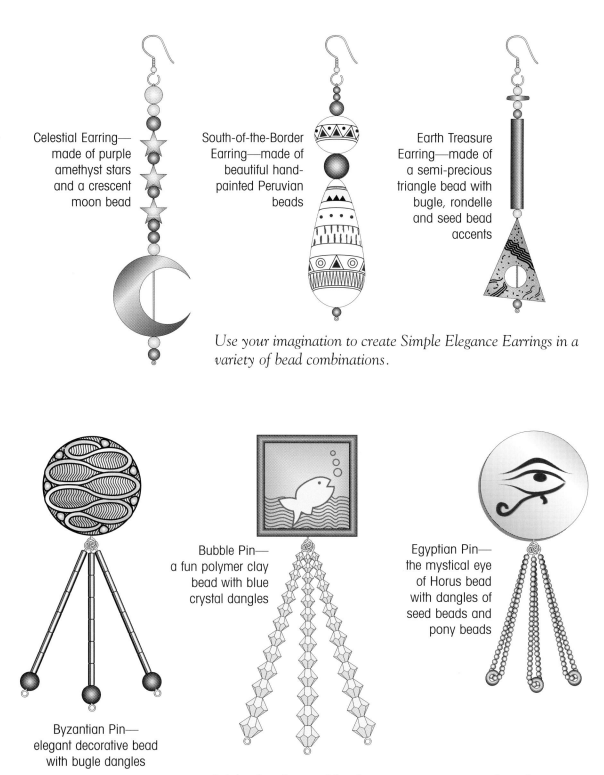

Celestial Earring—
made of purple
amethyst stars
and a crescent
moon bead

South-of-the-Border
Earring—made of
beautiful hand-
painted Peruvian
beads

Earth Treasure
Earring—made of
a semi-precious
triangle bead with
bugle, rondelle
and seed bead
accents

Use your imagination to create Simple Elegance Earrings in a variety of bead combinations.

Byzantian Pin—
elegant decorative bead
with bugle dangles

Bubble Pin—
a fun polymer clay
bead with blue
crystal dangles

Egyptian Pin—
the mystical eye
of Horus bead
with dangles of
seed beads and
pony beads

Make dangle pins like the Venetian Ice Brooch to liven up favorite outfits or add a bit of whimsy to just about anything in your closet.

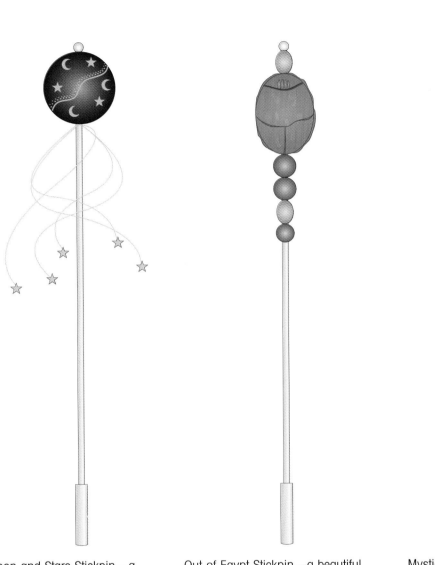

Moon and Stars Stickpin—a
Czechoslovakian bead with a
celestial motif and star dangles

Out of Egypt Stickpin—a beautiful
stickpin with coral and lapis bead
accents

Mystical Ethnic Stickpin—an eye
trade bead with painted wooden
bead accents

*Just a few interesting beads and a little design work can produce
these easy, elegant stickpins.*

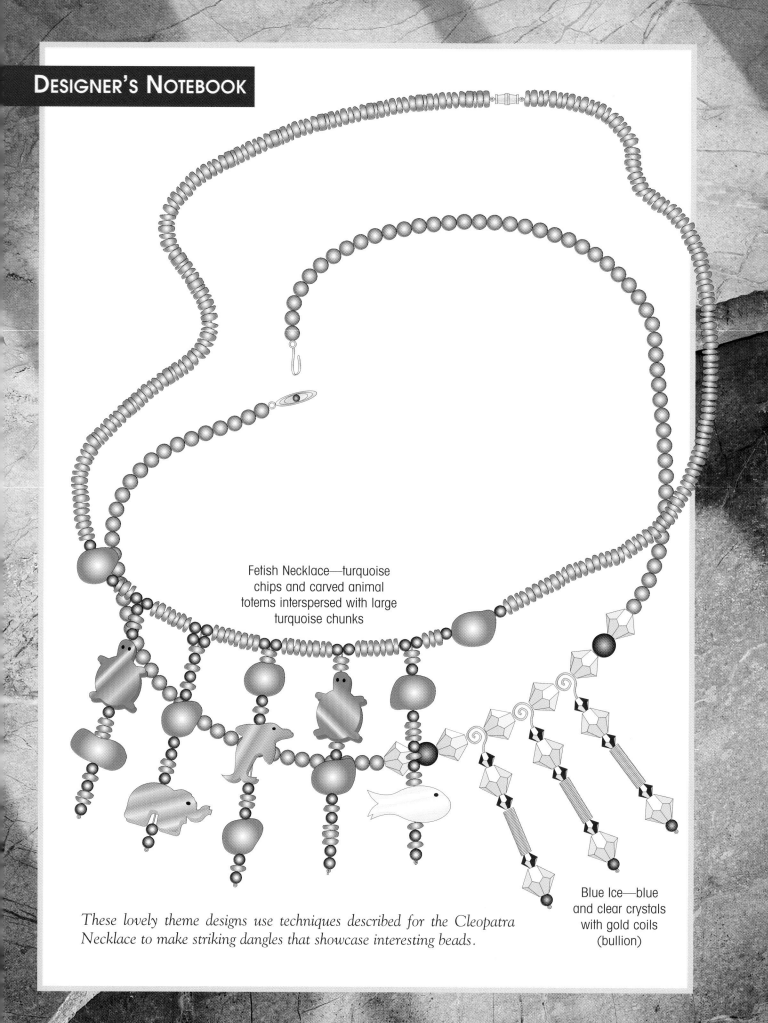

Fetish Necklace—turquoise chips and carved animal totems interspersed with large turquoise chunks

Blue Ice—blue and clear crystals with gold coils (bullion)

These lovely theme designs use techniques described for the Cleopatra Necklace to make striking dangles that showcase interesting beads.

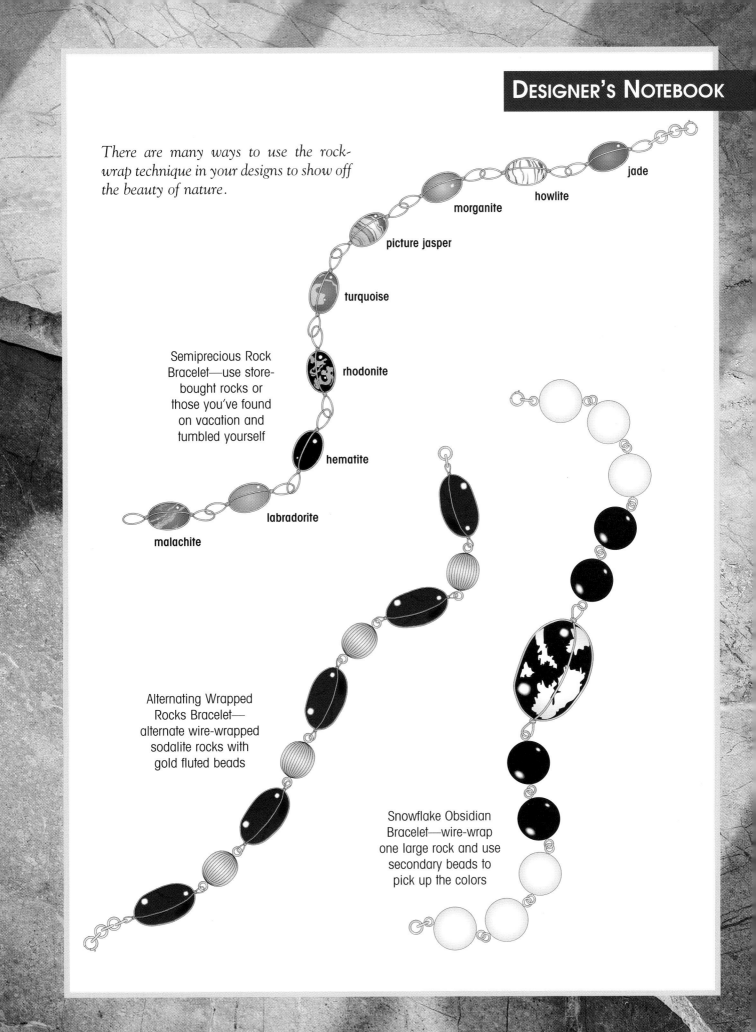

There are many ways to use the rock-wrap technique in your designs to show off the beauty of nature.

jade

howlite

morganite

picture jasper

turquoise

Semiprecious Rock Bracelet—use store-bought rocks or those you've found on vacation and tumbled yourself

rhodonite

hematite

labradorite

malachite

Alternating Wrapped Rocks Bracelet—alternate wire-wrapped sodalite rocks with gold fluted beads

Snowflake Obsidian Bracelet—wire-wrap one large rock and use secondary beads to pick up the colors

CHAPTER 3
BEAD STRINGING

Bead stringing is one of the easiest ways to produce good-looking custom jewelry. In this chapter, a two-needle technique is used to create the Ladder Stitch Choker. You'll find a simple method for adding adornments in the Triple Pendant Necklace project. The glittery Starburst Necklace ends in tiara-like points, and Lucky Pennies Necklace uses a unique dropped triangle shape. You may show off some favorites from your bead collection in the Beaded Skeleton Watch, and if you are up for a challenge you may wish to display your beading prowess by making the exquisite Phoenix Rising Fringe Necklace.

ℒADDER STITCH CHOKER AND TRIPLE PENDANT NECKLACE

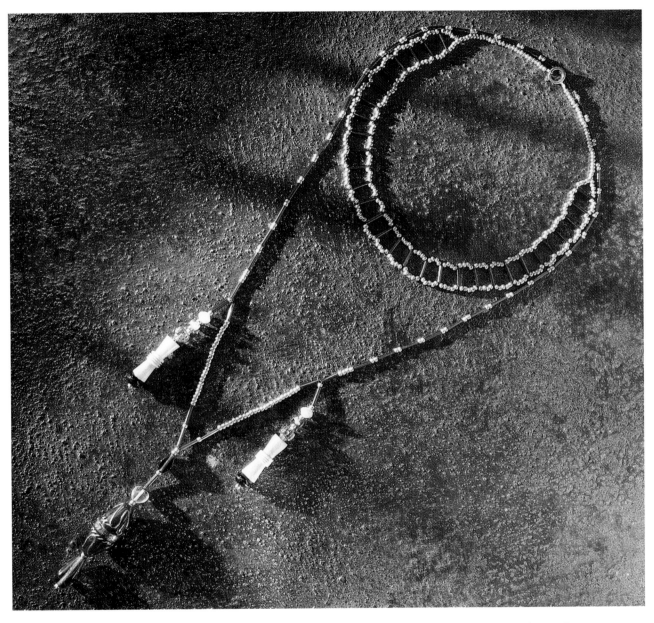

The choker is worked in ladder stitch using two needles at the same time. The long, slip-over-your-head Triple Pendant Necklace takes a simply strung necklace and adds side interest with two extra pendants. Notice the unusual combination of fancy and ethnic beads. Check out the Designer's Notebook pages at the end of the chapter for some inspiring variations of these two pieces.

MATERIALS

1 tube cobalt blue bugle beads, #3

1 tube gold seed beads, size 11/0

1 gold spring ring clasp

A variety of interesting beads (I used a Czechoslovakian lampwork bead, 2 large carved horn beads, 2 light blue lantern beads, and blue glass beads in assorted sizes and shapes)

TOOLS AND SUPPLIES

Scissors

Nymo thread

2 beading needles, #12

Clear fingernail polish

Long quilting pin

Padded Board

TECHNIQUE

LADDER STITCH CHOKER

1. Cut two 36″ lengths of Nymo thread. Add a needle to each thread. Tie the two thread ends together in a knot and pin to a padded board.

2. On the left-hand thread string 5 seed beads. On the right-hand thread string 4 seed beads. Then insert the left-hand needle through a bugle (Figure 3.1a). Now insert the right-hand needle through the same bugle going in the opposite direction (Figures 3.1b and c). *Note:* Try not to pierce the left-hand thread with the right needle.

3. Continue adding seed beads (5 left, 4 right) and a bugle as you did in Step 2 until you achieve the length you desire. (The 15″ choker pictured uses 30 bugles.)

AT-A-GLANCE

MAKING A CHOKER NECKLACE FIT

For a choker to fit comfortably around the neck, the inside edge of the necklace (the edge worn toward the neck) must be smaller than the outside edge. Thus, the inside edge in the Ladder Stitch Choker is strung in segments of four seed beads and the outside edge in segments of five seed beads.

4. After you have added the last bugle add 5 more seed beads on the left and 4 more on the right. Knot the thread ends together. String 28 gold beads on

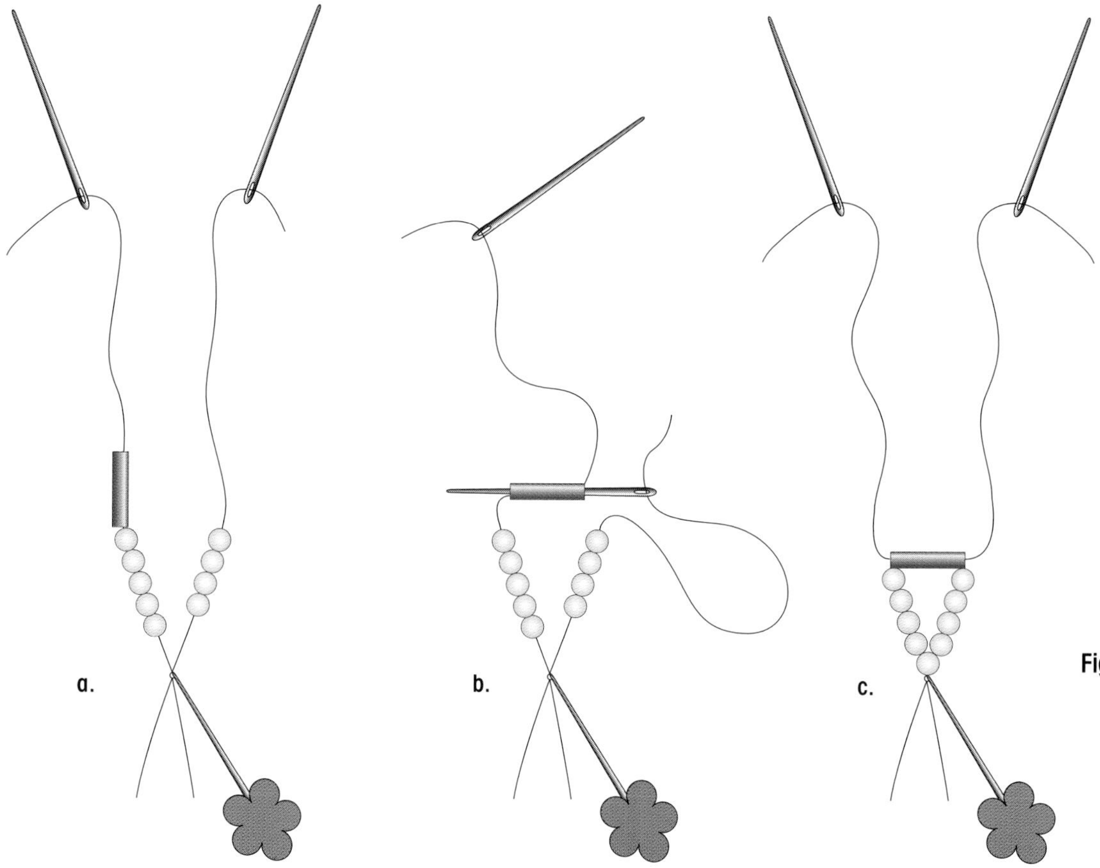

a.

b.

c.

Figure 3.1

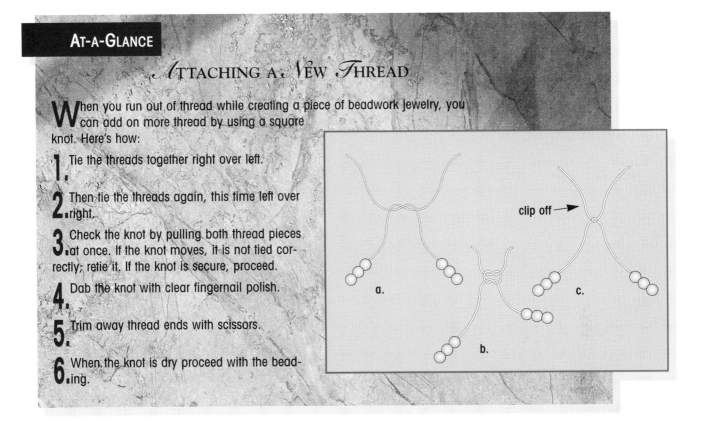

AT-A-GLANCE

ATTACHING A NEW THREAD

When you run out of thread while creating a piece of beadwork jewelry, you can add on more thread by using a square knot. Here's how:

1. Tie the threads together right over left.

2. Then tie the threads again, this time left over right.

3. Check the knot by pulling both thread pieces at once. If the knot moves, it is not tied correctly; retie it. If the knot is secure, proceed.

4. Dab the knot with clear fingernail polish.

5. Trim away thread ends with scissors.

6. When the knot is dry proceed with the beading.

clip off →

a.

b.

c.

one of the threads. Tie on the spring ring clasp (Figure 3.2) according to instructions on page 19. Dab knots with clear fingernail polish. Weave the other thread end back through the strung beads and cut off all excess thread ends.

5. Cut a 20″ length of thread. Tie the unfinished end of the necklace onto this thread at the thread's center point (Figure 3.3a). String 28 gold beads on one half of the thread, then tie on the jump ring (Figure 3.3b). Take the remaining long section of thread through the strung beads. Dab the knots with clear fingernail polish and cut off all excess threads.

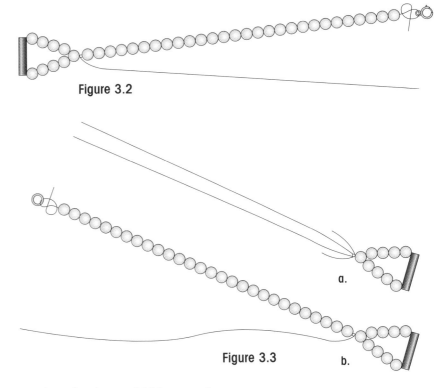

Figure 3.2

Figure 3.3

a.

b.

TRIPLE PENDANT

1. Cut a 40″ length of thread and add a needle. (This

pendant finishes at 33″ long and will slip over your head; if you wish to make it shorter you will need to add a clasp.)

2. Wind one end of the thread around a long pin and stick it in a padded board.

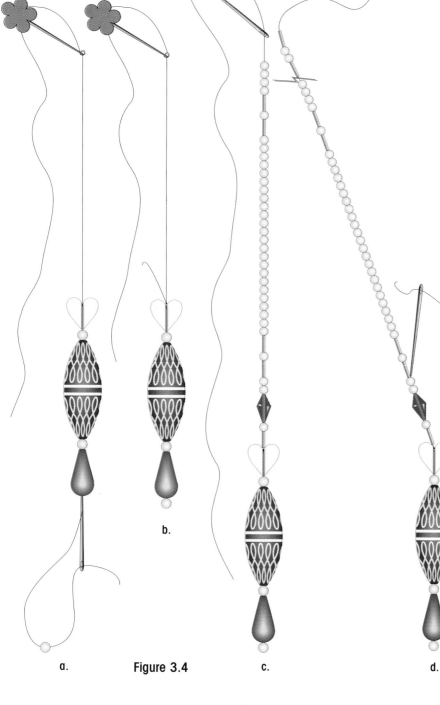

b.

a.   **Figure 3.4**   **c.**   **d.**

4. Add a needle to the remaining long end of thread and string 1 bugle, 1 gold seed, 1 blue glass bead, 2 gold seeds, 1 bugle, 1 gold seed, 1 bugle, 24 gold seeds, 1 bugle, 1 gold seed, 1 bugle, 4 gold seeds (Figure 3.4c).

5. Now string 1 bugle and 2 gold seed beads. Repeat this three-bead pattern 36 times.

6. Add 1 bugle, 24 gold seeds, 1 bugle, 1 gold seed, 1 bugle, and then insert the needle into the two seed beads that you strung next to each other at the beginning of Step 4 (see Figure 3.4d). Tie off the thread. Dot the knot with clear fingernail polish. Work the remaining thread through strung beads and then cut off any excess thread.

7. To add the other two pendants cut a length of thread 30″ long. Add a needle.

8. String 1 blue rondel and 1 gold seed. Reinsert the needle through the rondel and tie off the beginning thread (Figure 3.5). Dot the knot with clear fingernail polish. Cut off the thread tail.

a.

Figure 3.5

b.

3. String 1 heart-shaped bead, 1 gold seed, 1 lampwork bead, 1 gold seed, 1 teardrop bead, 1 gold seed. Now reinsert the needle through the teardrop (Figure 3.4a) and back through the rest of the strung beads

(Figure 3.4b). Remove the pin and tie off the thread close to the heart-shaped bead. Seal the knot with clear fingernail polish and then cut off the short excess thread.

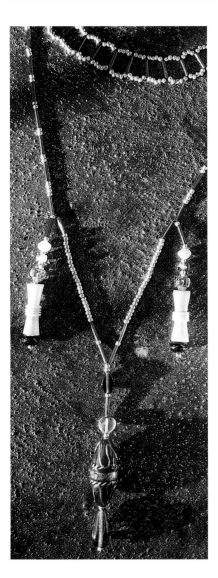

9. String 1 horn bead, 1 gold seed, 1 blue lantern, 1 gold seed, 1 blue glass bead, 1 gold seed, 1 blue/white bead, 1 gold seed, 1 bugle.

10. Insert the needle through the first single gold seed bead beyond the length of gold seed beads on the main structure strand (Figure 3.6). Work the thread through all of beads on the structure strand that are strung in the three-bead pattern described in Step 5 until you reach the last single gold seed bead before the length of gold seed beads. Bring the needle out of this gold seed bead.

11. String the pattern used on the other pendant but in reverse (that is, do Step 9 in reverse). Then add the rondel and the gold seed. Reinsert the needle through the rondel, bypassing the gold seed. Tie off and seal the knot with clear fingernail polish. Work thread through strung beads. Cut off any excess thread.

Figure 3.6

STARBURST NECKLACE

Silver-lined beads combined with color-shot crystals give this necklace an astral feeling. This piece also reminds me of the prismatic effect of sunlight shining through ice crystals. This 18″ long necklace falls at the hollow of the throat. For other design suggestions using the techniques described for this piece, see the Designer's Notebook pages at the end of the chapter.

main structure strand

Figure 3.7

MATERIALS

1 tube of silver-lined beads, size 8/0

54 faceted crystal beads with imbedded color layers, 8mm

1 silver clasp

TOOLS AND SUPPLIES

Scissors
Needle
Thread
2 long quilting pins
Padded board
Clear fingernail polish

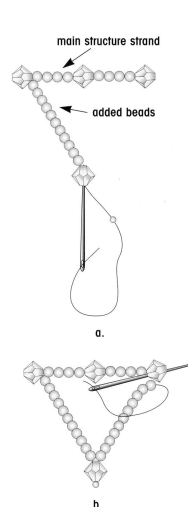

main structure strand

added beads

a.

b.

Figure 3.8

TECHNIQUE

1. Cut a 24″ length of thread. Add a needle.

2. String 1 crystal bead and 4 silver-lined beads. Repeat this five-bead pattern 34 more times, then add 1 more crystal. This creates the main structure strand. (See Figure 3.7.)

3. Wind the thread ends of the structure strand around the large quilting pins and insert them into a padded work surface.

4. Cut a 36″ length of thread. Add a needle.

5. Go through the first crystal bead on the main structure strand (leaving a tail of thread to tie off with), then add 11 silver-lined beads, 1 crystal bead, and 1 silver-lined bead. Reinsert the needle through the crystal bead on the new section, bypassing the last silver-lined bead you strung (Figure 3.8a). Now add 11 silver-lined beads.

6. The rest of the pointed sections are created the same way. Repeat Step 5, going through every other crystal on the main structure strand (Figure 3.8b). There will be a total of 18 pointed sections.

7. Finish off the necklace by adding the clasp (see page 19 for instructions). Seal the knots with clear fingernail polish.

ℒUCKY PENNIES NECKLACE

From the first moment I saw these special disc-shaped (linsin) beads, I loved them. The beads are made of brown glass with a thick copper plating on one side. Because two-sided beads can flip to either side at any time, you'll get a different configuration of matte brown and flashy copper beads each time you wear this piece. A linsin bead is a flattened shape with the hole running from side-to-side. Currently on the market there is a lovely celestial bead with incised stars and moons that would make good use of this stringing technique. For other ideas, see the illustrations of this kind of necklace in the Designer's Notebook section at the end of the chapter.

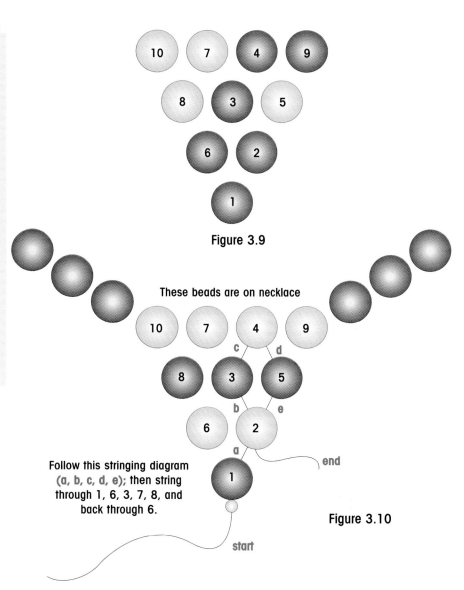

Figure 3.9

These beads are on necklace

Follow this stringing diagram
(a, b, c, d, e); then string
through 1, 6, 3, 7, 8, and
back through 6.

start

end

Figure 3.10

MATERIALS

24 disc-shaped (linsin) beads

1 tube copper-colored seeds beads, size 11/0 (or select a color to match the disc-shaped beads you have chosen)

1 tube gold seed beads, size 11/0

Nymo thread

1 gold filigree clasp

Clear fingernail polish

TOOLS AND SUPPLIES

Scissors

Beading needle, #12

TECHNIQUE

1. Cut a 24″ length of thread; add a needle.

2. String 3 gold seeds, 6 copper seeds, * 1 disc, 1 gold seed, 6 copper seeds, 1 gold seed. Repeat from the * 16 more times, then add 1 disc, 6 copper seeds, and 3 gold seeds.

3. Add the clasp (one part of the clasp on one end of the structure strand, the other part of the clasp on the other end) following the instructions on page 19. Work the thread ends back through the strung beads and cut off excess thread.

4. Cut another 24″ length of thread and add the needle. Consult Figure 3.9 for the placement of the disc-shaped beads. Note that the beads numbered 10, 7, 4, and 9 are located on the center front of the part of the necklace you have already

created. (Remember, the beads can flip from one side to the other, so the configuration of copper and brown sides vary from figure to figure.)

5. Now consult the stringing diagram in Figure 3.10. Note that in the following instructions (in Step 5 only) the word "seeds" after a disc is added refers to this pattern: 1 gold seed, 6 copper seeds, 1 gold seed. Insert the needle through disc #1, leaving a 12″ thread tail;

then add seeds. Add disc #2, seeds, disc #3, seeds, then go through disc #4 (on the strung necklace) and the first gold seed; now add 6 copper seeds. *Note:* When two sections of seed beads are strung to one disc, use only 1 gold seed bead. Now insert the needle through disc #5, add seeds, go through disc #2, and tie off the thread.

6. Place a needle on the thread tail coming out of disc #1. Add 1 gold seed bead

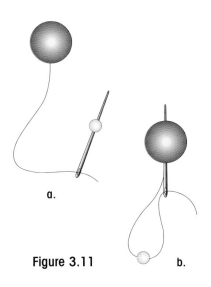

Figure 3.11

a.

b.

and reinsert the needle through disc #1 (Figure 3.11). This finishes off the bottom of the ornament.

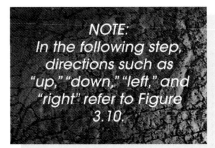

NOTE:
In the following step, directions such as "up," "down," "left," and "right" refer to Figure 3.10.

7. Now take the needle through the already-strung gold bead that is between discs #1 and #2 and closest to disc #1. Add 6 copper seeds, 1 gold seed bead, disc #6, 1 gold seed, and 6 copper seeds. Go through the gold seed that is already in place below disc #3, and without removing your needle, go through disc #3 and the gold seed in place on the other side of disc #3. Add 6 copper seeds, add 1 gold seed and go through disc #7 on the strung necklace. Go through the first gold seed to the left of disc #7 and then add 6 copper seeds, 1 gold seed, disc #8, 1 gold seed, and 6 copper seeds.

8. Now go through the gold seed bead already in place above disc #6 and then through

disc #6. Tie off the thread and work the thread through a few beads. Cut off any excess.

9. Now cut a 6˝ length of thread. Tie the thread below disc #5. Add a needle to the other end of the thread. Go through disc #5 and the already-strung gold seed, add 13 copper seeds, and then go through the gold seed below disc #9 and then disc #9 on the strung necklace. Bring the needle out and tie the thread to the beaded string. Knot it and then work the end through several beads on the strung necklace. Cut off any excess thread.

10. Follow the directions in Step 9 to complete the beading between disc #8 and disc #10.

BEADED SKELETON WATCH

ake a simple elegant watch face (I choose a skeleton watch face with the workings exposed) and turn it into stunning jewelry using a wide variety of beads from your collection. Work out a design that complements the watch face. I like the two-tone (gold/silver) look since the watch can then coordinate with any other jewelry. If you like you can add amulet charms to the beaded strands—notice the flippy little hummingbird on the piece in the picture. Check out the Designer's Notebook pages at the end of the chapter for some other ideas for setting off watch faces using interesting beads and beadwork.

*M*ATERIALS

Watch

Assorted beads in a variety of shapes, colors, and sizes

Charms, amulets (optional)

1 tube gold seed beads, size 11/0

2 gold fluted beads, 8mm

1 gold toggle clasp

*T*OOLS AND SUPPLIES

Scissors

Nymo thread

Beading needle, #12

BOND 527 cement

Quilter's Cut n' Press II or ruler and padded board

Long quilting pin

TECHNIQUE

1. First measure your wrist. Add 1″ to this measurement for wearing ease.

2. Lay the watch on the Quilter's Cut 'n Press II and plan out your beading design (based on the measurement in Step 1). Work out a layout with variety using some of the same beads on either strap to create a continuity of design.

3. Cut a 15″ length of thread. Add the needle. String beads in the desired pattern, add four gold seed beads, and then take the needle over and around the spring bar. Reinsert the needle through the first of the four seed beads (Figure 3.12). Then take the needle back through all of the strung beads. Repeat this step for the other two beaded strands on this side of the watch. Wind the beaded thread ends around the long quilting pin and insert it in the padded board.

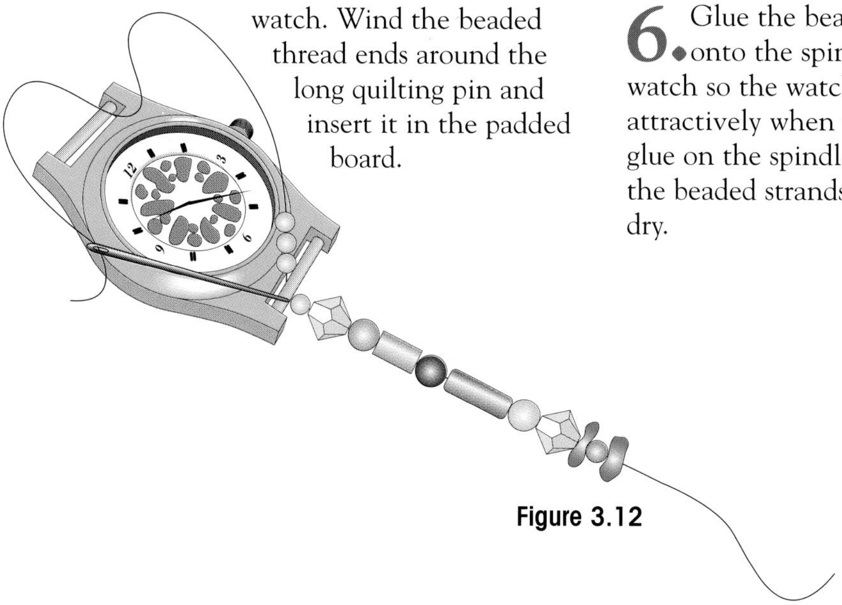

4. Work the other side of the band repeating Step 3.

5. Place the thread ends through the large fluted gold bead (Figure 3.13). Knot. (This is easier if you moisten the thread ends and twist them together.) Then knot the thread ends on one part of the clasp. Take the thread ends back through the large gold bead. Cut away excess thread. Place glue into both ends of the large gold bead. Let dry. Repeat for the other side of the beaded watch band, attaching the thread ends to the other part of the toggle clasp.

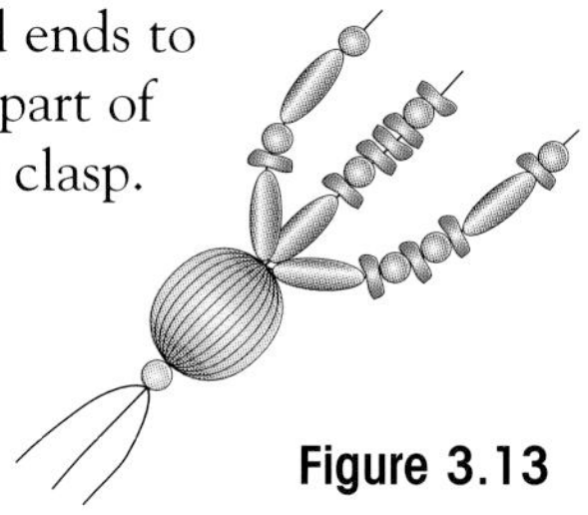

Figure 3.13

6. Glue the beaded strands onto the spindle of the watch so the watch will hang attractively when worn. Place glue on the spindle and arrange the beaded strands in place. Let dry.

Figure 3.12

PHOENIX RISING FRINGE NECKLACE

Beautiful strands of beads work up into a magnificent winged creature. The piece is made of Japanese beads accented with one exquisite ruby glass bead. I've designed this piece at a choker length of 16″ so it lays at the base of the throat. Look for other designs using this beading technique in the Designer's Notebook pages at the end of the chapter.

𝓜ATERIALS

Japanese Delica beads: 1
    tube each of black, blue-
    violet, lavender, light blue,
    turquoise, khaki, bronze,
    silver (antique),
    emerald/gold (luster)
1 tube bronze seed beads,
    size 11/0
1 ruby glass bead, 5mm
2 gold knot covers (bead tips)
2 gold jump rings, 4mm
1 gold lobster claw clasp

𝓣OOLS AND SUPPLIES

1 spool thread
Beading needle, #12
Clear fingernail polish
3 long quilting pins
Padded board
Jewelry pliers
BOND 527

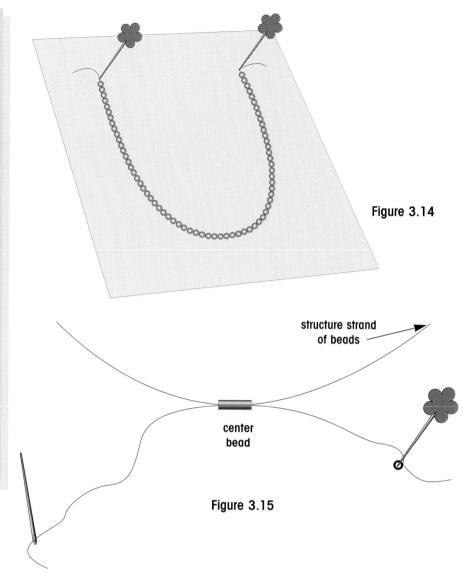

Figure 3.14

structure strand
of beads

center
bead

Figure 3.15

TECHNIQUE

1. Cut a 24″ length of thread. Add the needle. String 15½″ of blue-violet beads. Wrap each end of the thread around one of the long pins and pin the beaded structure strand to a padded board (Figure 3.14).

2. Cut another 24″ length of thread. Add the needle. Go through the center bead of the structure strand (Figure 3.15). Leave an 8″ tail and wrap it around another pin. Pin to the padded board.

3. Using the bead chart in Figure 3.16, begin by beading the center fringe of the necklace. (You will work the right half of the phoenix first, then the left half; the bead chart shows the right half.) String on the center fringe beads in the order shown. *To create the fringe:* At the end of each strand reinsert the needle

back through the strung beads, skipping the bottom silver bead (Figure 3.17). Run the needle through the strung beads back to the main structure strand. Tighten the string so there are no gaps in the beadwork. Insert the needle to the right through the next bead on the structure strand (Figure 3.18).

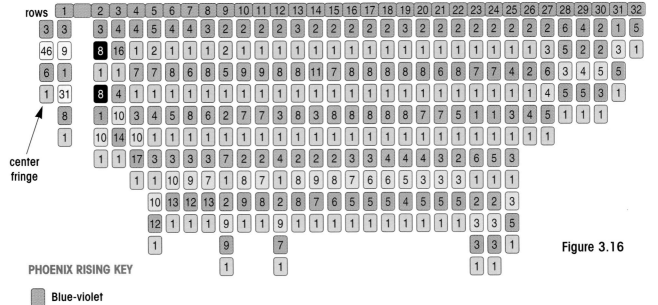

Figure 3.16

PHOENIX RISING KEY

- Blue-violet
- Khaki
- Turquoise
- Black
- Lavender
- Light blue
- Silver
- Emerald and bronze mix

Numbers refer to number of beads in that color

4. *To begin:* String on beads according to row 1 of the chart. Finish the strand of fringe as you did for the center strand in Step 3. Once the needle is back at the main structure strand, go through two beads (Figure 3.19). *Note:* This is the only time (once for each half) you will go through two beads; this is done to accommodate the bronze beads to be added later.

All other times you will take the needle through only one bead, as shown at the top of the bead chart.

5. Work all of the fringe as shown on the chart. Anytime you get down to 5″ of thread, tie on a new 24″ length of thread using a square knot. (See instructions for attaching a new thread on page 29.)

6. When the beading on this side of the winged creature is complete, tie off the thread on the main structure strand and work the remaining thread through the other structure

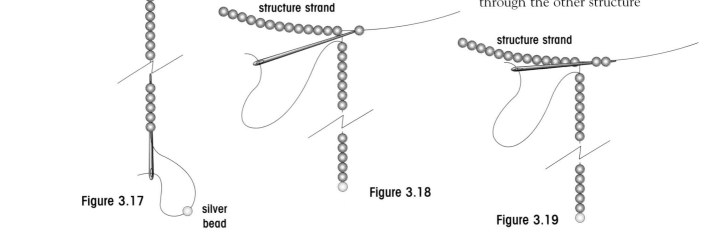

structure strand

Figure 3.17

silver bead

structure strand

Figure 3.18

structure strand

Figure 3.19

AT-A-GLANCE

Adding a Knot Cover

1. Insert the threaded needle through the hole between the two clamshells of the knot cover. String one seed bead. Take the needle through the seed bead twice (in the same direction) making sure the bead lies close to the metal knot cover. Knot the thread.

2. Place a dash of glue (BOND 527) in the bottom of the knot cover.

3. Close the knot cover with pliers. Let the glue dry, then cut away the excess thread.

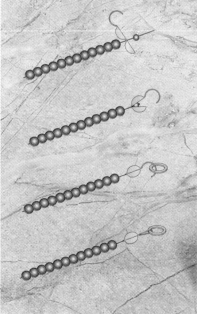

strand beads. Cut off any excess thread.

7. Untie the thread wound around the pin at the center of the motif. Attach another 24″ of thread. Repeat rows 1 through 32 on the chart for the other (left) side of the winged creature. Finish off as you did in Step 6.

8. To add the central ornament, cut a 20″ length of thread. Add the needle. String on 4 bronze seed beads, 1 ruby bead, 4 bronze seed beads (Figure 3.20). This is the topmost ornament. Now you will create the two fringes.

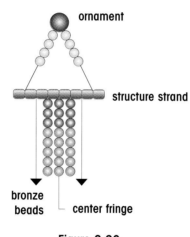

Figure 3.20

9. * Bring the needle through the bead that you skipped when making the fringe on the main structure (see Step 4). Add

40 bronze beads and 1 silver bead. Skip the silver bead and work the thread back through 2 bronze beads. Tie a knot. Work the rest of the thread through the strung beads. Cut away excess thread. This creates one of the hanging fringes. Repeat from the * on the other side of the center fringe to create the other fringe strand.

10. To finish the necklace: Remove the long pin. Knot the thread to the last bead. Dot with clear fingernail polish. Add a knot cover (see box). Add a jump ring to the loop on one of the knot covers; add a jump ring and the lobster claw clasp on the other end (see instructions on page 21).

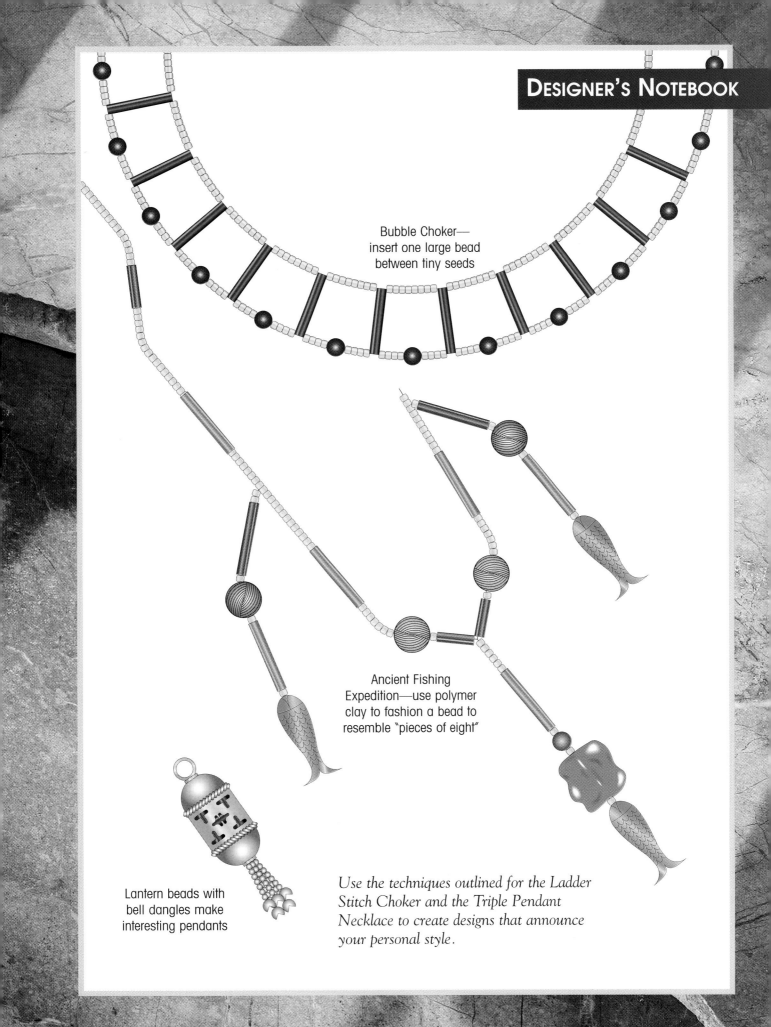

Bubble Choker—
insert one large bead
between tiny seeds

Ancient Fishing
Expedition—use polymer
clay to fashion a bead to
resemble "pieces of eight"

Lantern beads with
bell dangles make
interesting pendants

*Use the techniques outlined for the Ladder
Stitch Choker and the Triple Pendant
Necklace to create designs that announce
your personal style.*

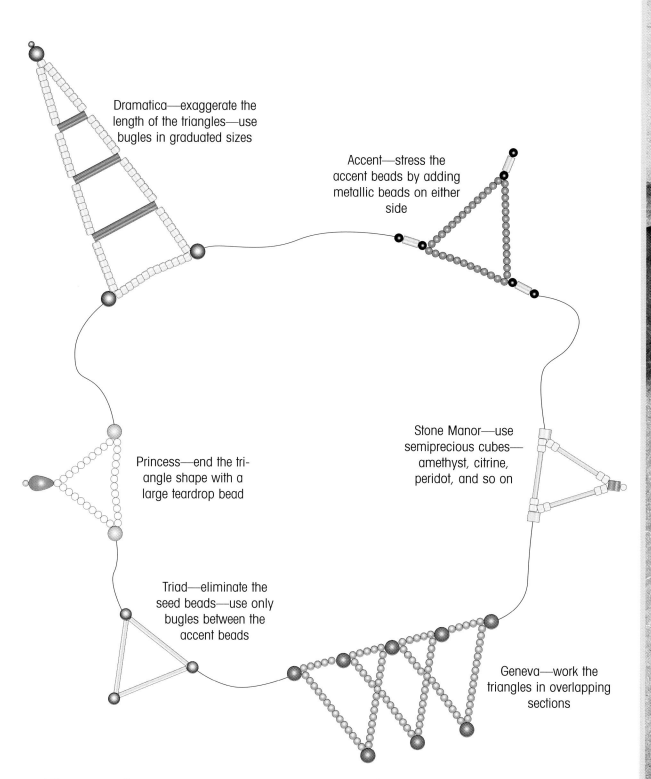

Dramatica—exaggerate the length of the triangles—use bugles in graduated sizes

Accent—stress the accent beads by adding metallic beads on either side

Princess—end the tri-angle shape with a large teardrop bead

Stone Manor—use semiprecious cubes—amethyst, citrine, peridot, and so on

Triad—eliminate the seed beads—use only bugles between the accent beads

Geneva—work the triangles in overlapping sections

There are endless ways to create stunning pieces using the techniques presented for the Starburst Necklace.

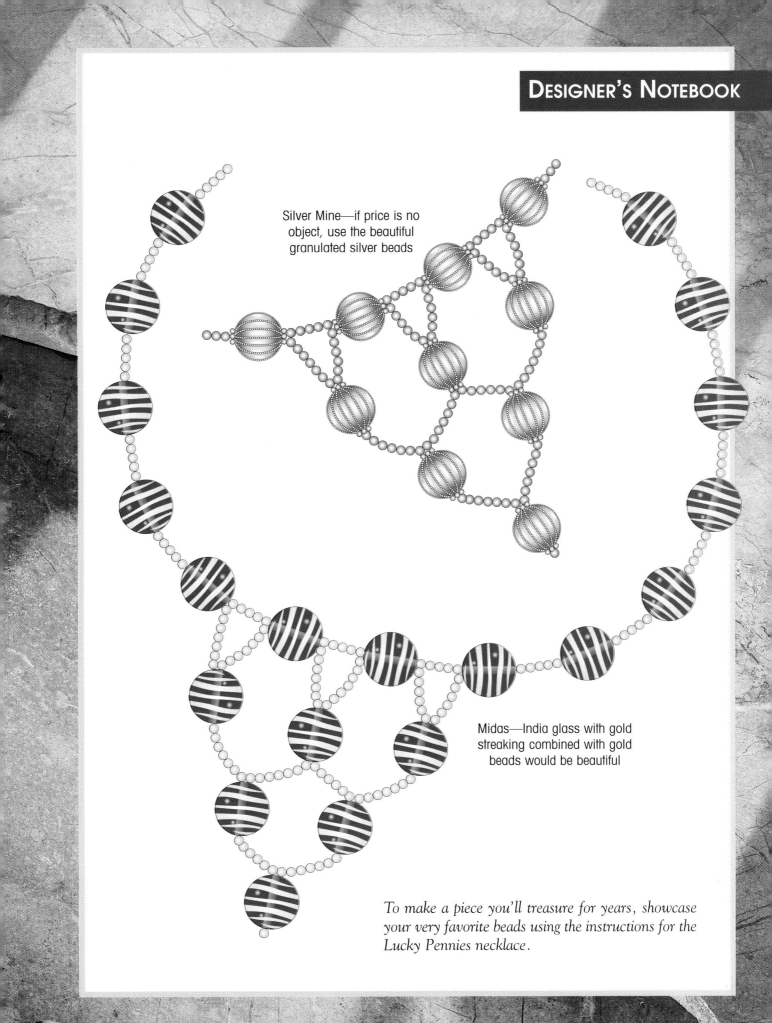

Silver Mine—if price is no
object, use the beautiful
granulated silver beads

Midas—India glass with gold
streaking combined with gold
beads would be beautiful

*To make a piece you'll treasure for years, showcase
your very favorite beads using the instructions for the
Lucky Pennies necklace.*

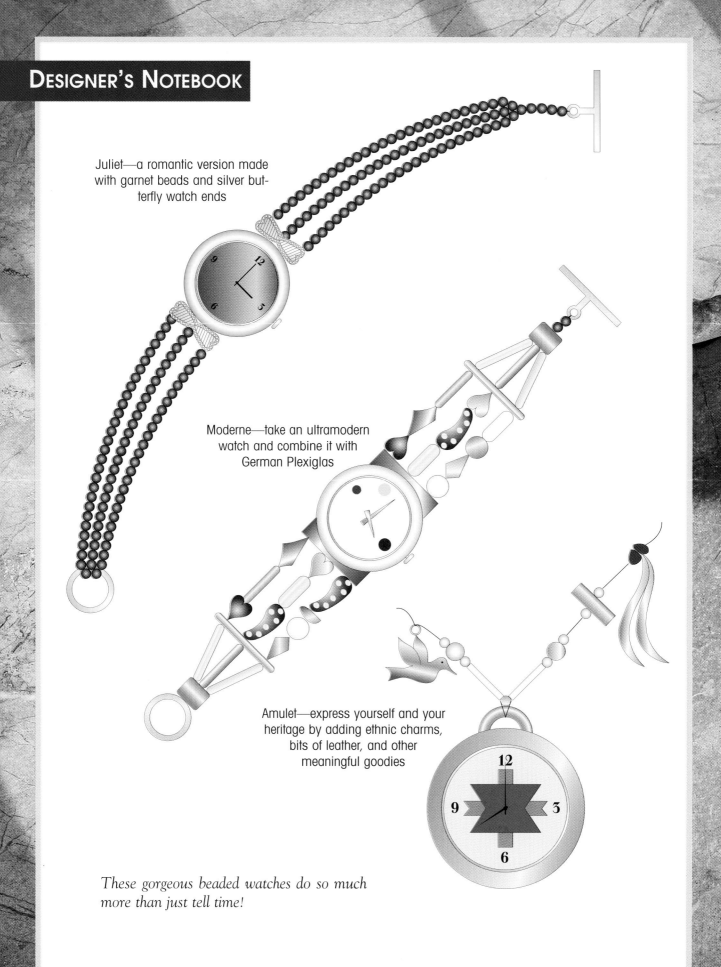

Juliet—a romantic version made with garnet beads and silver butterfly watch ends

Moderne—take an ultramodern watch and combine it with German Plexiglas

Amulet—express yourself and your heritage by adding ethnic charms, bits of leather, and other meaningful goodies

These gorgeous beaded watches do so much more than just tell time!

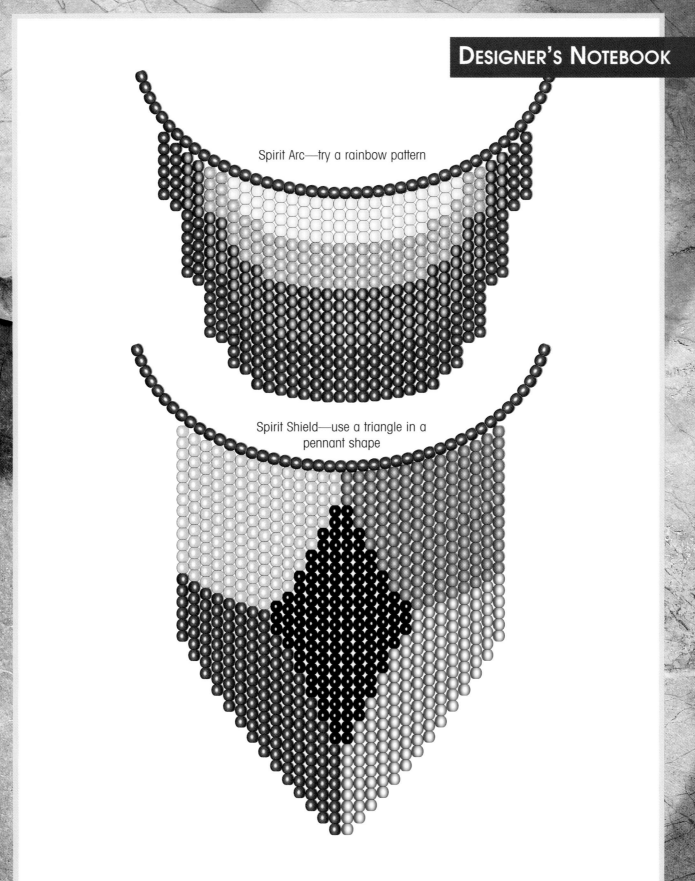

Spirit Arc—try a rainbow pattern

Spirit Shield—use a triangle in a
pennant shape

*Use the techniques described for the Phoenix Rising Fringe Necklace to create fringe patterns
that reveal other shapes and forms.*

CHAPTER 4
BEADING ON A GROUND

Using a needle and thread in a straightforward stab stitch you can attach beads to a ground or stable surface. The beautiful Beaded Picture Cabochon is sewn to an oval of soft leather. The Contempo Triangle Pin is built up upon a bed of wool felt. This sleek piece would be excellent on the lapel of a power suit. Flight of Fantasy takes the Victorian technique of card beading and reinterprets it in a contemporary fashion. This piece is so attractive you'll enjoy wearing it with a simple black dress to your next gala.

BEADED PICTURE CABOCHON

MATERIALS

Picture jasper cabochon, 20mm × 30mm

1 tube copper seed beads, size 11/0

1 tube silver seed beads, size 11/0

Piece of soft leather, 1¾" × 3"

Pin back, ¾"

TOOLS AND SUPPLIES

Oval template (available at art supply stores)

Scissors

527 BOND cement

Beading needle, #12

Thread

Permanent marker

Picture jasper is an exciting, naturally occurring stone that can be cut and polished to reveal shapes that suggest an abstract painting. Some people instantly see an intriguing mountain landscape in the cabochon pictured—what do you see?

The cabochon in this piece is attached to a piece of soft leather and surrounded by copper and silver seed beads to pick up the colors in the picture jasper. To get additional ideas for creating your own designs, see the illustrations in the Designer's Notebook pages at the end of the chapter.

TECHNIQUE

1. Trace around the cabochon onto the leather. Select a template opening about ½" larger all around than the cabochon tracing. Mark the template size with permanent marker. Remove the template. Glue the cabochon in place on the leather and let it dry overnight. Do not cut the leather.

2. Thread the needle and knot the end. Bring the needle up through the back of the leather as close to the cabochon as possible. String on enough seed beads to fit around the outside of the cabochon

(Figure 4.1). (If you wish, you can use two colors of seeds as in the piece pictured, coordinating the seed beads so they work with the colors of the picture jasper.)

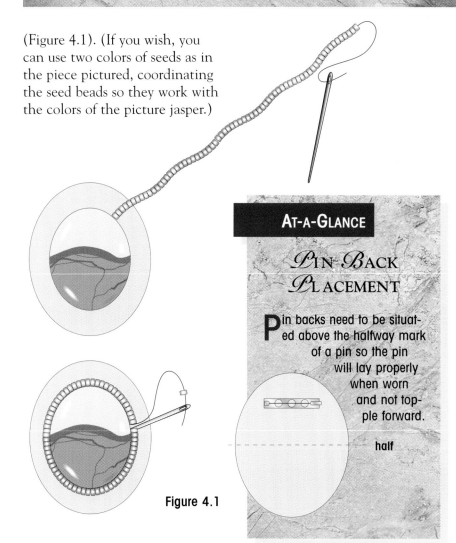

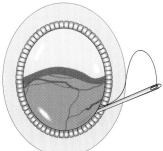

Figure 4.2

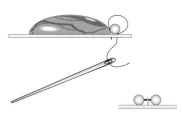

side view of couching

Figure 4.3

Figure 4.1

AT-A-GLANCE

Pin Back Placement

Pin backs need to be situated above the halfway mark of a pin so the pin will lay properly when worn and not topple forward.

half

3. Reinsert the needle through the leather next to the first strung bead (Figure 4.2). Knot the thread but do not cut it. Couch the beads in place around the cabochon as follows: Insert the needle through the leather so you come up close to the cabochon. To catch the string of beads, pass the needle over the string and then stab the needle back down through the leather close to where the thread had just come up through the leather (see Figure 4.3). Repeat this every 5 or 6 beads and continue couching the strand of beads surrounding the cabochon until you come full circle.

4. Add another strand of beads and couch it in place just outside the first strand. Trim the leather close to the second string of beads. Be careful not to cut any couching threads or the needle thread.

5. String on another ring of beads; couch. Tie off.

6. Using the template, mark and cut another oval of leather. Glue the leather oval on the back of the beaded piece and let it dry.

7. Glue the pin back on the back of the piece (see box) and let it dry.

CONTEMPO TRIANGLE PIN

MATERIALS

1 tube shiny black opaque
    seed beads, size 14/0
1 tube opaque red seed
    beads, size 12/0
1 tube transparent brilliant
    yellow seed beads, size
    11/0
White wool felt, 3" × 4½"
    (use two layers of craft felt
    if you are unable to find
    wool felt)
White silk, 3" × 4½"
Fusible web, 3" × 4½"

TOOLS AND SUPPLIES

Scissors
Beading needle, #12
Quilting thread
Tracing paper
Carbon paper
Pencil

TECHNIQUE

1. Trace the rounded triangle pattern pictured in Figure 4.4. Pin the pattern onto the felt and cut out the shape. Transfer the beadwork design onto the felt using the carbon paper. Fuse the fusible web to the silk according to the manufacturer's directions. Cut out the silk using the triangle pattern. This silk piece is used for the backing. Be sure to cut the triangle so the webbing will be on the inside. Set silk aside.

This modern design uses wool felt as the ground for the beading. A handful of seed beads are used to fill the shape. I used matte opaque beads, shiny opaque beads, and sparkly transparent beads to create contrast within the design. There are so many things you can do with this beading technique. For more great ideas, see the examples in the Designer's Notebook section at the end of the chapter.

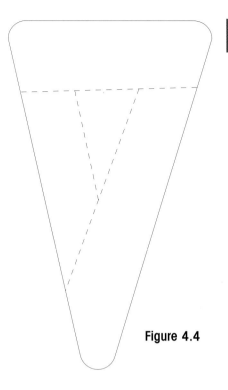

Figure 4.4

Beaded Coil Edging

1. Insert the threaded needle on the back of the piece.

2. Bring the needle to the front and add on enough beads to cover the raw edge. The coils should sufficiently cover the edge without being too "baggy."

3. Reinsert the needle from the back coming up very close to the previous stitch.

4. Continue the beaded coil edging around the entire piece.

5. To finish, knot the thread in between the layers and cut away excess thread.

2. Thread your needle and knot the thread end. Following the diagram in Figure 4.5, bead the defining lines of the design using the brilliant yellow beads. Bring the needle up from the back of the felt close to the edge of the triangle. Add enough beads to reach all the way across the triangle. Reinsert the needle into the felt. Bring the needle up to the next line (to the right of the central triangle section), add beads to reach the bottom. Reinsert the needle into the felt. Bring it back up to work the final short line (to the left of the central triangle section). Add beads. Bring needle to the back and knot. Cut off excess thread.

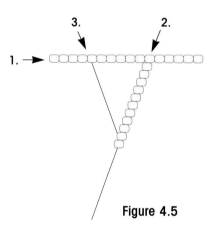

Figure 4.5

3. Rethread the needle. Bring the needle up to the top of the central black beaded triangle section. Add enough black beads to make a line straight across without the background show-

ing. Insert the needle to the back. Bring the needle up next to the first line. Add beads and reinsert needle. Continue until the central triangle section is filled.

4. Fill each of the other sections of the triangle with red beads using the same technique described in Step 3.

5. Fuse the white silk triangle to the back of the beaded piece following manufacturers's instructions.

6. Work the beaded coil edging as described in the box.

7. Sew the pin back in place (see box on page 50).

FLIGHT OF FANTASY NECKPIECE

MATERIALS

1 large unlined index card

Size 11/0 seed beads: 1 tube each of light gold, opaque white, transparent cobalt, transparent emerald; 2 tubes of opaque black

2 black bugle beads, #2

1 tube transparent bugle beads, #3

1 feather ornament spray (available in craft stores)

1½ yards black satin rattail cord

2 gold beads ½" long for cord endings

1 piece black felt, 3" × 4"

TOOLS AND SUPPLIES

Quilting thread

Beading needle, #12

E-6000 glue

Pencil

1 sheet typing paper

C ard beading was extremely popular during the Victorian era. You may still find stunning examples of this craft on antique lampshades; lamplight makes the richly beaded shades glow. Flight of Fantasy is a contemporary piece of jewelry with a sweet nuthatch motif and a feathered ornament. The long satin neckcord drapes down your back when the jeweled piece is close to the throat. You can adjust this striking piece to hang lower if you choose. Let your imagination take flight as you design card-beaded pieces that reflect your interests and tastes. The illustrations in the Designer's Notebook section at the end of the chapter can provide some inspiration.

TECHNIQUE

1. Trace the design motif pictured in Figure 4.6 onto a piece of typing paper. Turn the sheet over and rub a pencil across the entire back of the design. Center the typing paper motif right side up on the index card. Now trace the motif with a

AT-A-GLANCE

Card Beading Tips

1. Work any small design elements first (such as the bird's beak in this piece) to make sure you have the exact placement.

2. Try not to make too many needle holes too close together because the index card can weaken and tear.

3. Work lines of beads whenever possible; then go back and couch the lines in place (see the discussion of couching on page 50).

4. Work the outline of a shape (like the bird's breast, done in opaque white beads) and then fill in with the rest of the beads.

5. Work the main motif first and then the background,

5. Cut the card to an oval shape, cutting as close as possible without cutting the stitching.

6. Cut an oval of black felt the same size as the beaded oval.

7. Find the center of the satin rattail cord and sew the cord in place on the back of the beaded oval (see Figure 4.7).

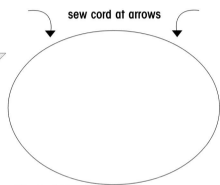

sew cord at arrows

Figure 4.7

8. Cut four feathers away from the ornament (two from each side). Set these feathers aside. Glue the feather ornament in place on the back of the beaded oval. Let dry.

9. Holding the black felt oval in place on the back of the beaded oval, begin the beaded coil edging (see instructions for this technique on page 52).

10. Dip the ends of the rattail cord in glue and insert each end into a gold bead. Insert the ends of two feathers into the other end of the bead. Let the piece dry thoroughly.

Figure 4.6

place for the bird's beak. Work the black beads on the bird's crown. Sew on the black eye bead. Work the opaque white on the head and breast, then on the tail feathers. Sew cobalt blue beads on the tail and the back.

pencil using a firm touch so the rubbed pencil transfers. Remove the paper. Do not cut the card.

2. Thread the needle with 18″ of thread. Knot the end. Sew the two black bugles in

3. Sew the branch on using the emerald green beads. Fill in with the gold background beads.

4. Create the border by sewing the transparent bugles in a radiating fan pattern around the entire piece.

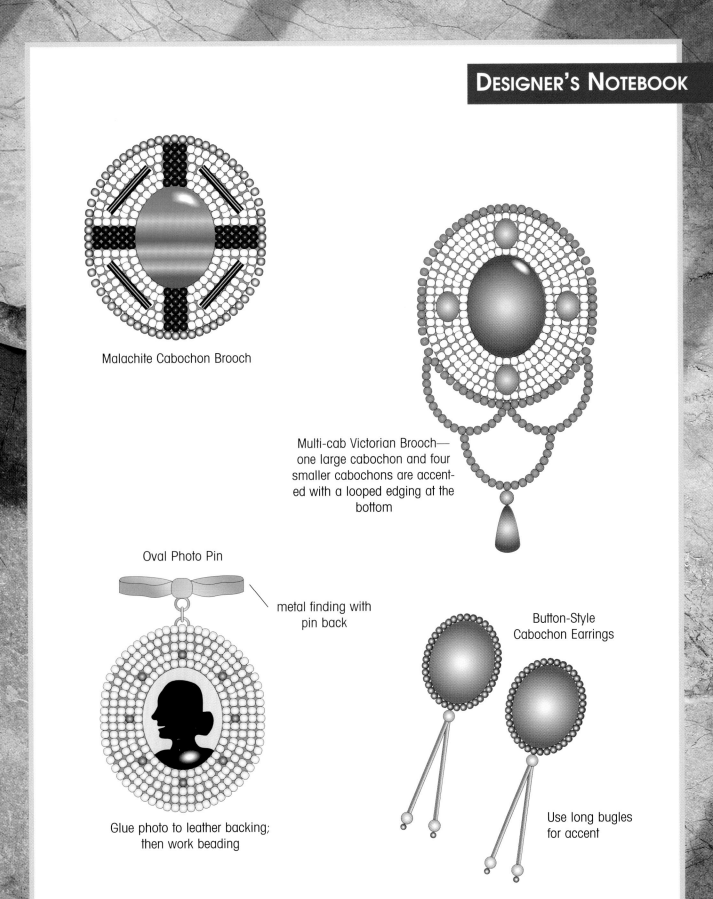

Malachite Cabochon Brooch

Multi-cab Victorian Brooch—
one large cabochon and four
smaller cabochons are accented with a looped edging at the
bottom

Oval Photo Pin

metal finding with
pin back

Button-Style
Cabochon Earrings

Glue photo to leather backing;
then work beading

Use long bugles
for accent

*Once you have mastered the Beaded Picture Cabochon, let your creativity flow as you find
ways to display other cabochons.*

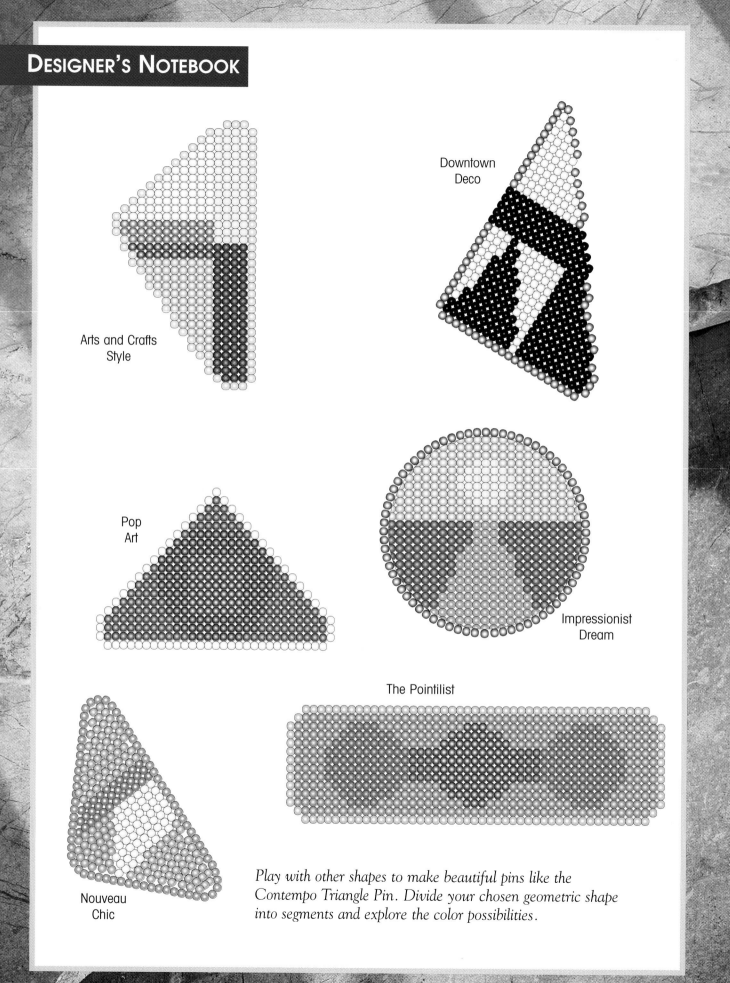

Arts and Crafts
Style

Downtown
Deco

Pop
Art

Impressionist
Dream

The Pointilist

Nouveau
Chic

*Play with other shapes to make beautiful pins like the
Contempo Triangle Pin. Divide your chosen geometric shape
into segments and explore the color possibilities.*

You can use any well-defined shape for Victorian card beading, the technique used for the Flight of Fantasy necklace project.

Elegant Butterfly Pin

Christmas Flowers—use 2mm beads in the center and surround with seeds

Tribal Graffiti Necklace—use tab shapes beaded in primitive spirals

CHAPTER 5

WOVEN BEADWORK

*C*reate sculptural forms of jewelry using bead-weaving techniques. A modern version of the old-fashioned daisy stitch is used for the elegant Garden Party Necklace. Brick stitch works up into a beautiful pair of Jeweled Diamond Earrings. Peyote stitch, a classic Native American beadwork technique, is used for the contemporary Peyote Snakeskin Bracelet and the elaborate Night Sky Peyote Pouch. This handsome neckpiece will become a family heirloom. Everyone will want it!

GARDEN PARTY NECKLACE

MATERIALS

1 hank opaque white seed
   beads, size 11/0
1 tube cornflower blue seed
   beads, size 11/0
1 tube gold seed beads, size
   11/0
1 gold toggle
2 frosted glass leaves
5 small gold jump rings, 4mm
1 large gold jump ring, 8mm
1 gold split ring, 6mm

TOOLS AND SUPPLIES

Jewelry pliers
Thread
Beading needle, #12
Clear fingernail polish

The daisy chain technique has been in use for a long time. Just two colors of seed beads are used. Be sure to select colors with enough contrast so the daisy motif is instantly identifiable. The Garden Party Necklace gathers a whole gardenful of daisies. The sleek toggle and frosted leaves ornament takes the piece uptown. Wear it with the leaves either in front or back. The necklace measures 17″, plus the 1¾″ toggle ornament. For other examples of how you can incorporate these innocent daisies into your designs, see the Designer's Notebook pages at the end of the chapter.

TECHNIQUE

> **NOTE:**
> In needle-weaving technique it is important to keep the tension consistent as you bead.

1. Thread the needle. String 8 white beads. Reinsert the needle through the first strung bead (Figure 5.1a). Add a blue bead (Figure 5.1b), then insert the needle through the fifth strung bead. String on a white bead. Now go through the sixth strung bead. Add a white bead, then insert the needle through the white bead to the left (Figure 5.1c). Now continue the pattern (Figure 5.1d).

2. The necklace shown is made of a very long string of daisy motifs gathered into four strands. Each strand is made up of 60 daisy motifs. This necklace contains 240 daisies. To make a necklace with one, two, or three strands simply multiply 60 times the desired number of strands.

3. To make the four-strand necklace group the 240 daises into four equal-length groups. Thread a needle and wrap the thread tightly around the threads of the grouped strands (two threads) twice. String on a gold seed bead. Go through the bead two or three times adding the circle section of the toggle. Tie off the thread.

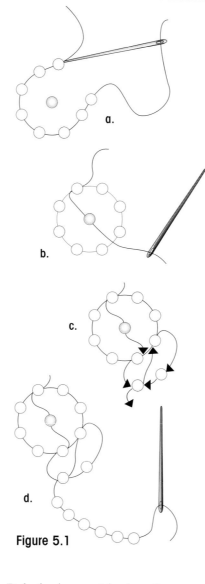

Figure 5.1

Dab the knot with clear fingernail polish. Repeat this thread wrap on the other side of the grouped beaded strands, but instead of adding the toggle piece add the split ring.

4. To the end with the split ring add the five small jump rings in succession (see instructions for adding jump rings on page 21). Then add the toggle stick.

5. To create the toggle ornament (Figure 5.2): Thread the needle with 18″ of thread. String 1 gold bead leaving a 5″ tail, then add a frosted leaf (point first) and 4 gold beads. Now go around the large jump ring and reinsert the needle back through the last gold bead. String on 3 gold beads, a frosted leaf (round side first), and a gold bead. Reinsert the needle through the leaf bypassing the gold bead. Tie off the thread. Dot with clear fingernail polish.

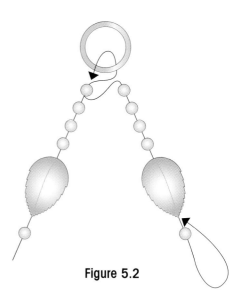

Figure 5.2

6. Add the needle to the thread tail. Insert the needle through the leaf bead, bypassing the gold bead. Tie off the thread. Dot the knot with clear fingernail polish.

7. Open the jump ring at the top of the ornament and place it on the toggle circle.

JEWELED DIAMOND EARRINGS

Brick stitch, also called Comanche stitch, produces a woven brickwork in which the beads lie in an offset pattern. I used a tube of transparent pony beads of many colors and separated them into piles of single colors. The earrings are worked in stripes of color creating a rainbow effect. The Designer's Notebook pages at the end of the chapter contain some other examples of beadwork featuring the brick stitch.

*M*ATERIALS

1 tube transparent pony
   beads in multicolors, size
   5/0 (to recreate the earrings shown you'll need 14
   bright blue, 24 pale pink,
   16 yellow, 18 purple, 8
   turquoise, 6 clear, and 10
   red)

1 tube metallic gray seed
   beads, size 12/0

Polyester quilting thread

2 beading needles, #12

Clear fingernail polish

French hook earring findings

*T*OOLS AND SUPPLIES

Jewelry pliers

TECHNIQUE

NOTE:
In needle-weaving
technique it is important to
keep the tension consistent
as you bead.

1. Cull the beads, discarding
any that are misshapen or
have too small a hole, and separate them into color piles. Note
that the earring construction
begins in the center row of the
diamond, in this instance with
the blue beads.

2. Cut a 30″ length of thread.
Add two blue beads. Add
one of the needles to a thread
end. Take the needle through
one of the beads so the beads lie
in a line (Figure 5.3).

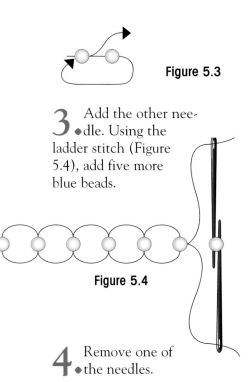

Figure 5.3

3. Add the other nee-
dle. Using the
ladder stitch (Figure
5.4), add five more
blue beads.

Figure 5.4

4. Remove one of
the needles.

5. Row 2: String one pale
pink bead. Bring the nee-
dle under the thread between
the first two blue beads (Figure
5.5). Bring the needle up and
add another bead (Figure 5.6).
Continue beading across.

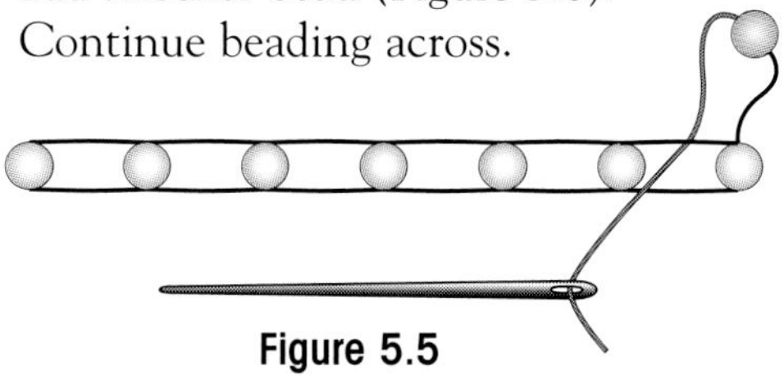

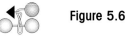

Figure 5.5

 Figure 5.6

6. Turn the piece at the end
of each line of beading,
working left to right, then right
to left. Continue adding each
row in the same manner.
(Follow the bead colors in the
color photo if you wish to make
earrings like the ones pictured.)

7. After you weave on the top
two red beads, string 12
metallic gray seed beads
to form a hanging
loop (Figure 5.7). Tie
off the thread. Dot
with clear fingernail
polish.

8. Add a nee-
dle to the
other thread
end and begin
working the bottom half of the
diamond using the brick stitch.
Tie off.

Figure 5.7

9. Create another beaded diamond using the above
technique.

10. Using the pliers, attach
the two French hook
findings.

PEYOTE SNAKESKIN BRACELET

MATERIALS

Regular pencil or 1/4" dowel
1 large tube golden yellow
   seed beads, size 11/0
2 gold cap ends
2 gold jump rings, 6mm
1 gold lobster claw clasp

TOOLS AND SUPPLIES

Beading needle, #12
Thread
10" nylon cord, 3/8" diameter
Clear fingernail polish
527 BOND cement
Masking tape
Jewelry pliers
Cigarette lighter

TECHNIQUE

NOTE:
In needle-weaving technique it is important to keep the tension consistent as you bead.

P eyote stitch is seen extensively in Native American bead-work. Instead of lying in rows, the beads are staggered, pro-ducing a beautiful pattern even when the stitch is worked in beads of a single color. This unique coil bracelet is worked over a pen-cil or dowel. The long, supple length of circular beading extends past the proposed length of the central cord, and thus when the beading is sewn in place on the cord it creates intriguing soft rolls with a rippled appearance (hence the name "snakeskin"). This sleek bracelet is 8″ in length. If you like this stitch, try some of the patterns illustrated in the Designer's Notebook pages at the end of the chapter—or create your own.

1. Cull the beads, discarding any that are distorted or have a hole that is too small. Thread 24″ of thread on the needle. Add enough beads to go around the pencil; this must be an even number (I used 12).

Leaving a 6˝ thread tail tie the strand of beads around the pencil. Secure the thread tail to the pencil with a piece of masking tape (Figure 5.8). This is row 1.

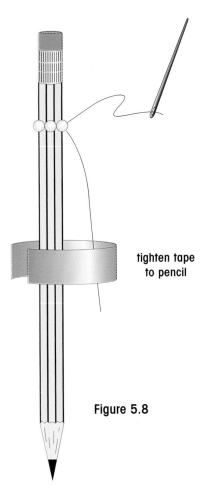

tighten tape
to pencil

Figure 5.8

2. Insert the needle through the first bead on row 1. Now string on a bead, then insert the needle through the second bead on row 1 (Figure 5.9). Add another bead, then take the needle through the next bead over on row 1. Notice how the beads are forming a staggered pattern of a single bead and two stacked beads. Continue creating this pattern until you insert needle back through the first bead of this new row. This is row 2.

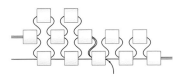

Figure 5.9

3. String on the first bead of the next row. Now take the thread through the next raised bead on row 2 and then string on a bead. Continue filling in the pattern to the end (see Figure 5.9).

4. Go through the first bead at the beginning of the row. Always go through the first bead of each row or the beading will go awry. Remember to keep your tension even (not too tight, not too loose) as you work or else the pattern won't appear correct.

5. The rest of the circular peyote pattern is worked by repeating row 2 (staggered beads) and row 3 (filling in between the staggered beads; see Figure 5.10). Work this pattern all of the way to the end of the pencil. Tie off leaving a 6˝ tail at the end.

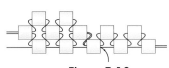

Figure 5.10

6. Remove the length of beading from the pencil. Set aside.

7. The nylon rope has a tendency to unravel, so hold the end of the cord with the pliers and fuse the end using a lighter. Wrap a piece of masking tape around the opposite end of the cord. Cement the cap end onto the fused end of the cord (Figure 5.11).

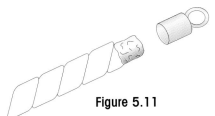

Figure 5.11

8. Place the beadwork tube on the cord. Push the beadwork back toward the end cap. Take the other end of the cord and hold it with the pliers. Cut off the masking tape end. (The finished cord should measure 7˝ with another ½˝ inserted into the end caps.) Fuse the end of the cord. Cement the end cap in place.

9. Add the needle to one of the thread tails. Sew the beadwork to the cord as close to the end cap as possible (Figure 5.12). Repeat for the other side.

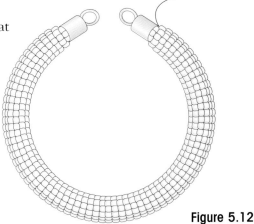

Figure 5.12

10. Attach a jump ring and the clasp to one of the end caps. Add a jump ring to the other end cap. (For instructions on adding jump rings, see page 21.)

NIGHT SKY PEYOTE POUCH

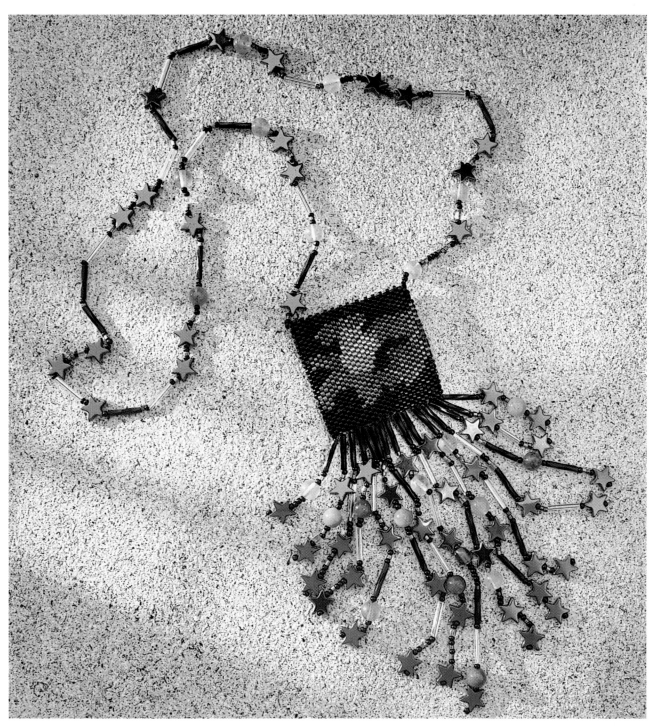

ost beaders love small amulet bags. An amulet bag can be worn as a striking neckpiece and can conceal small personal treasures. This piece was inspired by a dark stormy night sky when all of a sudden the clouds parted and a brilliant silver moon appeared. Moments later it was gone. The lavish fringe and hang strap are created of beautiful hematite stars, fancy agate, moonstone, and lush black twist bugles. The piece has a 22″ neck strap and measures 18″ when suspended from a jewelry hook. For other pattern ideas, see the illustrations in the Designer's Notebook pages at the end of the chapter.

MATERIALS

Japanese Delica beads: 2 tubes of black; 1 tube each of emerald, silver, and bronze

½ hank hematite stars, 6mm

12 fancy agate beads, 6mm

12 moonstone beads, 6mm

1 tube black twist bugles, size 5/0

1 tube silver-lined bugles, size 5/0

1 tube black seed beads, size 11/0

TOOLS AND SUPPLIES

Cardboard toilet tissue tube

Black Nymo thread

Beading needle, #12

Clear mailing tape

Clear fingernail polish

TECHNIQUE

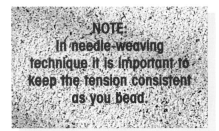

NOTE:
In needle-weaving technique it is important to keep the tension consistent as you bead.

POUCH

1. Cut a 24″ length of Nymo thread; add the needle. String 62 black beads. Tie the beads into a circle leaving a ¼″ section of thread without beads and a 6″ tail. For the following instructions, see Figure 5.13: Cut down the length of the tissue tube. Curl the tube enough to

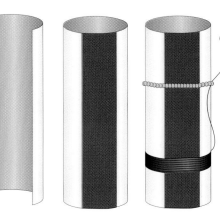

Figure 5.13

slip on the circle of black beads. Take the beads off and tape the tube in the position in which the beads fit correctly. Replace the circle of beads and tape the tail to the tube. This is row 1.

2. Go through the first strung bead, add a black bead, reinsert the needle through the second bead, add a black bead. Continue for the whole row. This will create a row of dropped beads. This is row 2.

3. Add 3 black beads on the needle. For some reason, if these beads are not added at this point, the beading becomes too tight (the beads will stick straight out and won't be able to be flattened against the tissue tube).

4. Insert the needle through the first bead of row 2; add a bead between the dropped beads. Insert the needle through the next bead. Add a bead. Continue for row 3. (See Figure 5.14.)

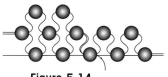

Figure 5.14

5. Continue alternating Steps 2 and 4 using the graph in Figure 5.15 as a placement guide for the different colored beads. Anytime you need to add a new thread use the method described on page 29.

6. When you have finished the pouch portion of the necklace, tie off the thread. Dot the knot with clear fingernail polish. Remove the cardboard tube. Add the needle to the thread tail at the bottom. Weaving the thread back and forth, sew the bottom of the bag together.

NECK STRAP

1. Cut a 60″ length of Nymo thread. Add the needle and work with the string doubled for added strength.

2. String beads in a pleasant design using an eclectic mix of bugle twists, moonstones, fancy agates, hematite stars, black seeds, silver-lined tubes, and Delicas left over from the pouch (Figure 5.16). * Work the thread through the beads at the side of the bag, then come back up the side; reinsert the needle back through the beads on the neck strap and tie off. Dot the knot with clear fingernail polish. Repeat from the * for the other end of the neck strap.

FRINGE

1. Because the fringe is strung in a continuous length, there are often problems with

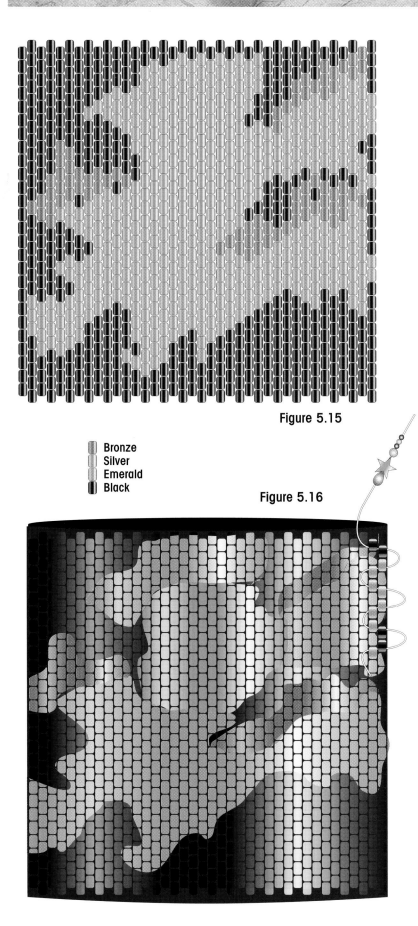

Figure 5.15

- **Bronze**
- **Silver**
- **Emerald**
- **Black**

Figure 5.16

thread breakage. To avoid broken thread and spilled beads, use lengths of thread that are long enough to create two lengths of fringe, and do not knot in the middle of a fringe. On my bag, the smallest fringe length is 1½″ at the sides and the longest fringe is the center strand, which is 4″.

2. All fringe strands start with a black twist bugle and end with a star and a black seed bead stopper. Use beads of your choice in the center of the strand of fringe. Make it a nice mix to add variety and visual interest.

3. Thread the needle. Work the thread through the beads on the pouch, bringing the needle out of a bead on the bottom edge where you want a fringe to appear. Add beads to make one length of fringe, starting with a black twist bugle and ending with a star bead and black seed bead stopper. Reinsert the needle through the star, bypassing the seed bead. Bring the needle back through all of the beads on the fringe strand. Bring the needle out at the next bead on the pouch where you want a strand of fringe to appear.

4. Work the fringe across the bottom. I used 15 strands.

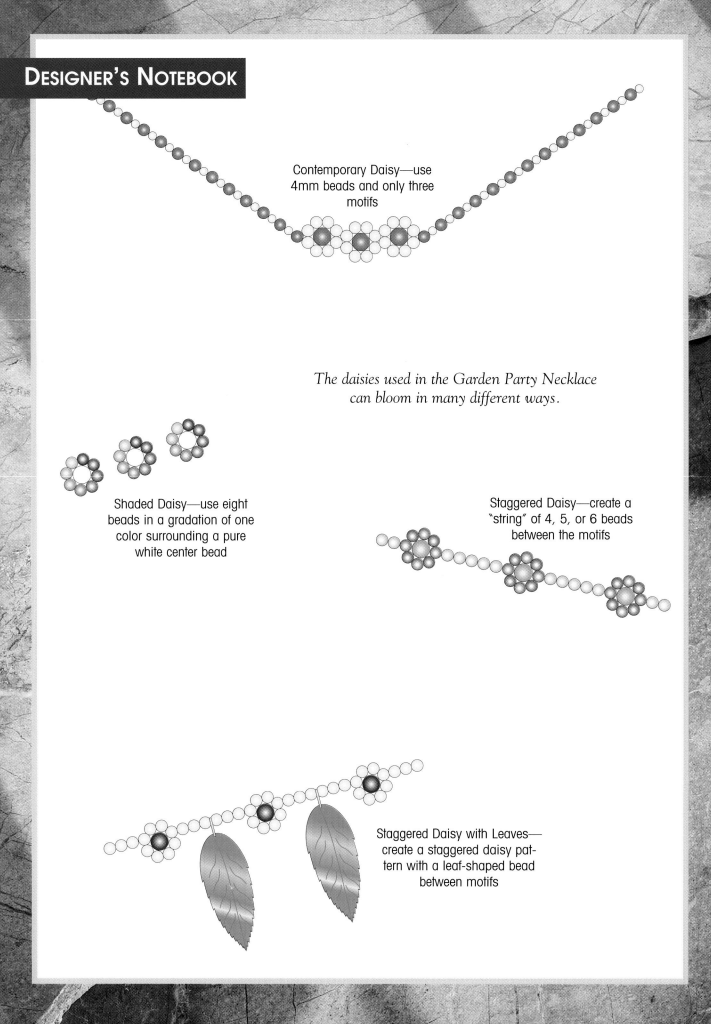

Contemporary Daisy—use 4mm beads and only three motifs

The daisies used in the Garden Party Necklace can bloom in many different ways.

Shaded Daisy—use eight beads in a gradation of one color surrounding a pure white center bead

Staggered Daisy—create a "string" of 4, 5, or 6 beads between the motifs

Staggered Daisy with Leaves— create a staggered daisy pattern with a leaf-shaped bead between motifs

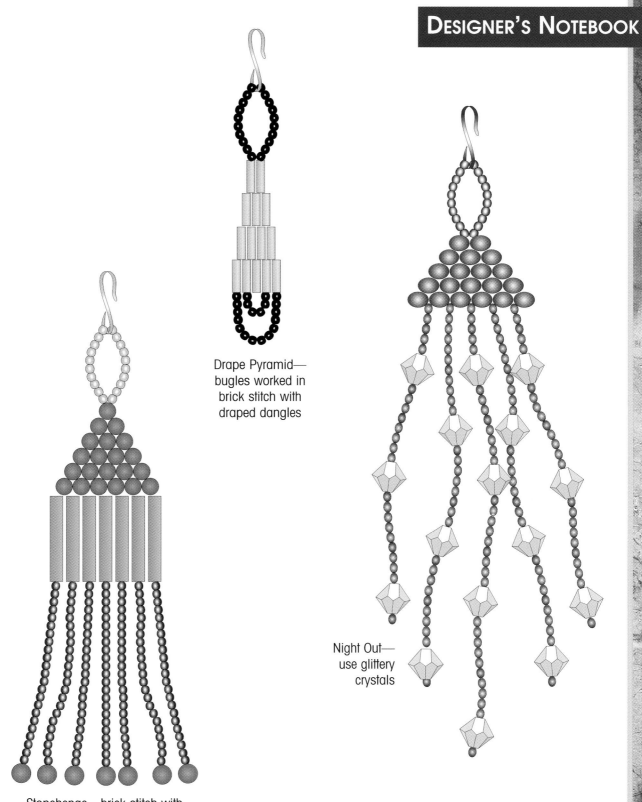

Drape Pyramid—
bugles worked in
brick stitch with
draped dangles

Night Out—
use glittery
crystals

Stonehenge—brick stitch with
bugle and seed bead dangles ending in a semiprecious stone

If you like the Jeweled Diamond Earrings you'll enjoy making up your own designs using the same technique.

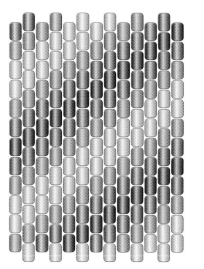

Try snakeskin patterning. The diagonal stripes are darkest in the center, graduating to an extremely light tone

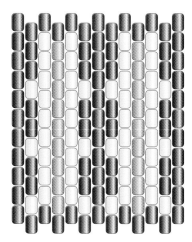

Here a vertical pattern is used. Notice the flower worked down the center. Try a traditional garden pallette or use vibrant colors

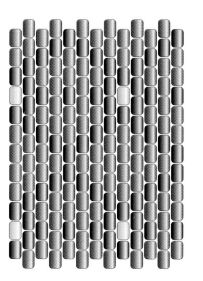

This unusual pattern would create a seam at the back of the piece. A transparent bead background with contrasting patterning would be beautiful

The Peyote Snakeskin Bracelet can be beaded in a variety of subtle and not-so-subtle patterns.

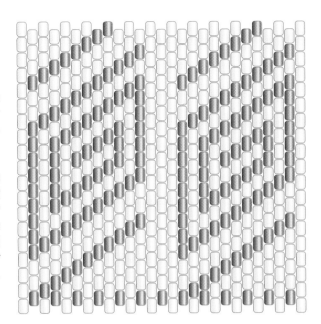

This dynamic design creates strong diagonals. A palette of soft pastels—baby blues and soft yellows—will tone down the pattern. Bold, strong colors—red, white, black, purple—will enhance the strong pattern. Since this is just one side of the bag (front or back), count the number of beads along the horizontal edge and double it to figure the total number of beads to begin with.

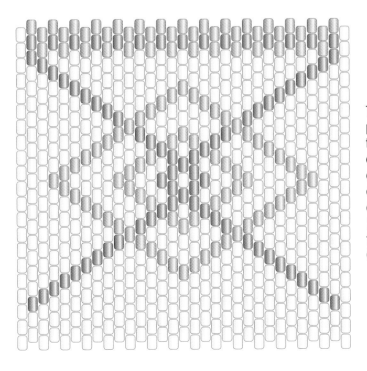

This is the lovely Celtic Knot pattern. Work it in colors that create a memory—the colors of a favorite painting, a beautiful piece of fabric, or a piece of hand-painted china. Make it in colors you love. The fringe could echo the triangle pattern in the Celtic Knot

The bead weaving technique used to make the Night Sky Peyote Pouch lends itself to intricate patterns and striking contrasts.

CHAPTER 6
POLYMER CLAY

Here's a wonderful selection of creations made with polymer clay. Mountain Music Necklace is a delightful piece with a Southwestern flavor. Real gold leaf is used to enhance the flower beads of the Gilded Bead Necklace. And finally, the lovely Sapphire and Sunshine Neckpiece shows how to manipulate polymer clay into sensuous organic forms.

culpey III, Fimo, and Cernit are the three major brands of polymer clays. Each has its advantages. Sculpey III is easy to find (it is manufactured in the U.S.) and comes in a wide variety of colors; Fimo, the popular European brand, seems to hold fine detail well; and Cernit is known for its permanence once baked. No matter which brand you purchase, always look for fresh bars by checking the elasticity of the packaged clay. Once polymer clays have dried in the package they become extremely crumbly and difficult to work with.

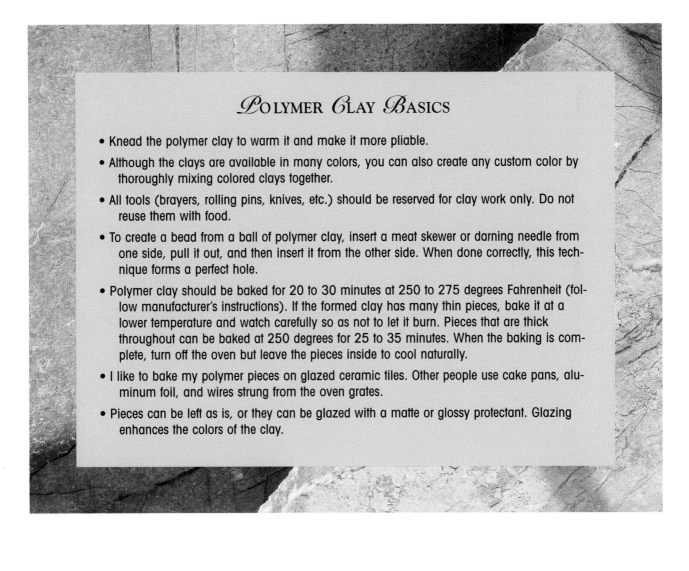

Polymer Clay Basics

- Knead the polymer clay to warm it and make it more pliable.

- Although the clays are available in many colors, you can also create any custom color by thoroughly mixing colored clays together.

- All tools (brayers, rolling pins, knives, etc.) should be reserved for clay work only. Do not reuse them with food.

- To create a bead from a ball of polymer clay, insert a meat skewer or darning needle from one side, pull it out, and then insert it from the other side. When done correctly, this technique forms a perfect hole.

- Polymer clay should be baked for 20 to 30 minutes at 250 to 275 degrees Fahrenheit (follow manufacturer's instructions). If the formed clay has many thin pieces, bake it at a lower temperature and watch carefully so as not to let it burn. Pieces that are thick throughout can be baked at 250 degrees for 25 to 35 minutes. When the baking is complete, turn off the oven but leave the pieces inside to cool naturally.

- I like to bake my polymer pieces on glazed ceramic tiles. Other people use cake pans, aluminum foil, and wires strung from the oven grates.

- Pieces can be left as is, or they can be glazed with a matte or glossy protectant. Glazing enhances the colors of the clay.

MOUNTAIN MUSIC NECKLACE

Symbolic interpretations of treasures found within mountains—turquoise, silver, and amber—are found in this 22˝ necklace. Sleek sections of wood create an interesting rhythm. For other ways to use polymer beads similar to those created for this piece, see the Designer's Notebook section at the end of this chapter.

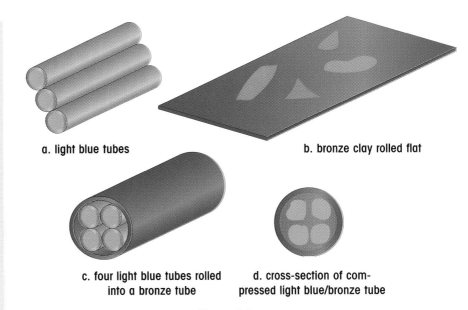

a. light blue tubes   b. bronze clay rolled flat

c. four light blue tubes rolled into a bronze tube

d. cross-section of compressed light blue/bronze tube

Figure 6.1

TECHNIQUE

MAKING THE BEADS

1. Roll the light blue clay into four tubes. Roll the bronze clay out flat. Lay the light blue clay tubes on the bronze clay. Compress the clays and roll the piece into a large tube. (See Figure 6.1.)

2. Roll the turquoise clay out flat. Roll a small piece of the orange clay out flat and cut it into irregular shapes. Place a few of the orange pieces here and there on the turquoise clay.

3. Lay the light-blue/bronze tube on the turquoise clay. Roll all of the clays into a tube.

4. With a utility knife, slice the tube into 1 piece approximately ¾" long and 12 pieces approximately ½" long. Roll each of the pieces into a ball and pierce to create a bead.

5. After cutting the beads, knead what is left of the tube until it turns a solid color (olive). Roll out two spheres slightly less than ½" in diameter. Pierce them to create beads.

6. Lay all the beads on the ceramic tile and bake at 250 degrees Fahrenheit for 20 to 30 minutes. When cool, glaze.

STRINGING THE NECKLACE

1. Thread a 36" length of thread on the needle. Then string the following: 1 small light amber, 1 small dark amber, 1 silver melon, 3 brown glass, 1 olive (clay), 1 silver melon, 1 small turquoise (clay), 1 brown glass, 1 small turquoise, 1 silver melon, 1 wooden tube, 1 silver melon, 1 brown glass, 1 small turquoise, 1 silver melon, 1 wooden tube, 1 silver melon, 1 brown, 1 small turquoise, 1 brown, 1 small turquoise, 1 silver melon, 1 large amber, 1 small turquoise, 1 large amber, 1 silver melon, 1 wooden tube, 1 silver melon, 1 small dark amber. Add the large turquoise bead for the centerpiece of the necklace. Now string the other half of the necklace by reversing the stringing pattern.

2. Add a jump ring and the clasp to one end of the necklace and a jump ring to the other end (see page 19 for instructions on adding a clasp). Tie off. Work the threads back through some of the beads. Cut away excess thread.

GILDED BEAD NECKLACE

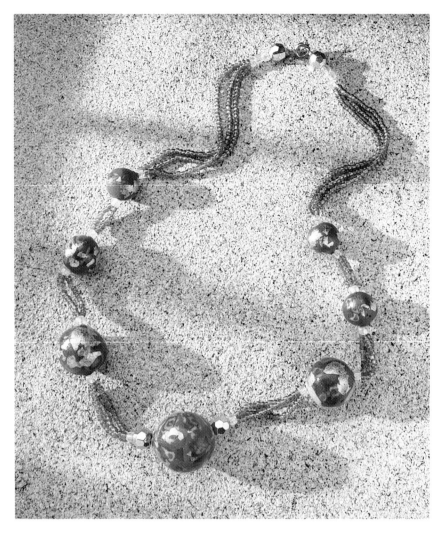

MATERIALS

Polymer clay: purple, hot pink, yellow, dark blue, orange, white

4 gold faceted beads, 10mm

20 iridescent pony beads

1 large tube light purple iris seed beads, size 11/0

1 gold clasp

1 page gold leaf

TOOLS AND SUPPLIES

Thread

3 beading needles, #12

Brayer

1 ceramic tile

Gloss glaze

Paintbrush

Skewer

Scissors

Clear fingernail polish

Long quilting pin

Padded board

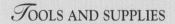

For this lovely piece, flower canes are rolled into beads and then gilded with real gold leaf. This unusual design uses both seed beads and polymer clay beads. This necklace finishes at 20″ long.

TECHNIQUE

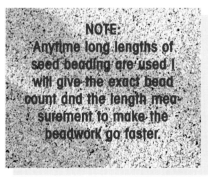

NOTE:
Anytime long lengths of seed beading are used I will give the exact bead count and the length measurement to make the beadwork go faster.

Figure 6.2

1. To create the seven beads in descending sizes out of purple clay (Figure 6.2): Roll one large bead, about ¾″ in diameter. Then roll two beads about ½″ in diameter. Finally, roll out four beads slightly smaller than the previous two.

2. Create flower canes by rolling the other colors of polymer clay into tubes. Stack the tubes as shown in Figure 6.3. Roll the stack back and forth so all clay pieces fuse into one long tube.

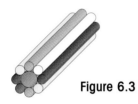

Figure 6.3

3. Slice the tube with a utility knife into ⅛″ pieces (Figure 6.4). Place the flower discs on the purple beads, covering as much of each bead as possible. Roll each bead once again so that the clay flowers become one with the bead.

Figure 6.4

4. Pierce the beads, then lay them on the tile and bake.

5. When the beads have cooled, apply the gloss and the gold foil to each bead as follows: Place a bead on a skewer (Figure 6.5) and glaze the entire bead with gloss protectant. Apply pieces of the gold foil to the bead before the glaze dries (use more glaze as needed to enable the gold to adhere). Now glaze the entire bead with gloss again to seal the bead and the foil (Figure 6.6).

6. Cut three 25″ lengths of thread. Add needles. Wrap the three thread ends around a long pin and insert it into a padded board.

7. On all three threads together string 1 gold bead and 3 ponies. Now separate the three threads and string 51 seed beads (3½″ strung) on each. Take all three threads through 1 pony, 1 small polymer bead, and 1 pony. Separate the threads and string 9 seed beads on each.

Take all three threads through 1 pony, 1 small polymer bead, and 1 pony. Separate the threads and string 12 seed beads on each. Unite the threads and string 1 pony, a ½″ polymer bead, and 1 pony. Separate the

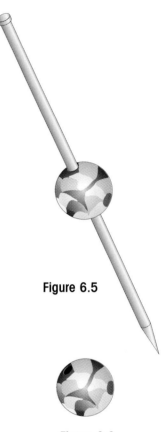

Figure 6.5

Figure 6.6

threads and string 22 seed beads (1½″ strung) on each strand. Take all three threads through 1 pony, 1 gold bead, and the large polymer bead.

8. Repeat the beading pattern (in reverse) for the other side of the necklace.

9. Tie on the clasp (see instructions on page 19). Knot the threads and work the thread ends back through the strung beads. Dot the knots with clear fingernail polish.

SAPPHIRE AND SUNSHINE NECKPIECE

n this unusual piece, exotic plaque-style beads are fashioned of folded clay ovals textured with cheesecloth. Plain and marbleized beads make up the side strings, which terminate in curved end horns. This neckpiece finishes at 22″ long. See the Designer's Notebook pages at the end of the chapter for ideas for making other unusual beads from polymer clay.

MATERIALS

Polymer clay: dark blue-
    purple, emerald green,
    sunshine yellow, violet
8 iridescent purple oval
    beads, 6mm × 4mm
2 gold end caps
1 gold spring ring clasp
2 seed beads, any color, size
    11/0
2 green wooden beads, 8mm
2 jump rings, 4mm

TOOLS AND SUPPLIES

Tracing paper
Pencil
Utility knife
Cheesecloth
Beading needle, #8
Carpet thread
Scissors
BOND 527 cement
Brayer
4 ceramic tiles
Wire, 6" length

TECHNIQUE

1. Trace the oval pattern given in Figure 6.7 and cut out the tracing.

Figure 6.7

2. Using the brayer, roll out the purple and green clay to a ⅛" thickness. Using the utility knife and the oval pattern cut out five ovals of each color of clay. Lay one layer of cheesecloth on each oval and roll across it with the brayer to create an interesting texture.

3. Pick up one of the purple ovals and gently fold it over lengthwise so the textured side is showing. Gently fold one of the green ovals in the same way. Abut the two folded ovals together along the long edge (Figure 6.8). Press them together

firmly but not so much that the oval shape is distorted. Repeat with the other ovals so you have five plaques.

4. Roll out a snake of purple clay ⅝" in diameter. Slice the snake into five ½" sections. Pierce each piece lengthwise to form a bead. Press each bead to the back of one of the plaques (see Figure 6.9 for placement).

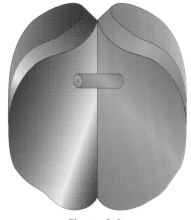

Figure 6.9

5. Roll out five yellow balls about ¼" in diameter. Press one ball onto the front of each plaque (Figure 6.10). Set the completed plaques on ceramic tiles in preparation for baking.

Figure 6.8

Figure 6.10

6. To make the beads: Roll six purple clay balls ½″ in diameter. Roll two ½″ balls and ten ⅜″ balls of yellow clay. Roll two violet balls ⅜″ diameter. Pierce all the beads and set them on ceramic tiles in preparation for baking.

7. To make marble beads: Combine equal parts yellow and green clay. Work the mixed clay until you achieve a marbled look; don't overwork the mixture or the colors will blend into a solid color. Roll the marbleized clay into six balls ½″ in diameter. Pierce each ball. Set the beads on a tile.

8. Create an end horn by rolling the green clay into a cone measuring 1¾″ long (Figure 6.11). Now make another one. Insert wire through each end horn and then carefully bend the wire to create a gently curved form (Figure 6.12). Take a single layer of cheesecloth and gently press it into each end horn to create texture. Set the end horns on a tile.

Figure 6.11

Figure 6.12

9. Bake all the pieces. Cool.

10. Check the plaques to see if all of the components have adhered properly. If they have not, discreetly glue the elements in place. Add a strip of glue on the bead attached to the back of the plaque for added protection.

11. To string the neckpiece cut a 28″ length of carpet thread. Add the needle. Go

twice with the thread through the seed bead and knot the thread.

12. String 1 end horn (narrow end first), 2 small yellow beads, 1 purple iridescent bead, * 1 small yellow, 1 marble, 1 purple iridescent. Repeat from the * three times. Then string 1 violet, 1 large yellow, 1 green wood, ** 1 purple, 1 plaque. Repeat from the ** four times. Then string 1 purple bead.

13. Work the other side of the necklace by repeating the beading pattern on the other side (in reverse). Be sure to place the end horn in the correct position (bottom first). Add the seed bead and knot. Cut off thread ends. Dab the knots with jewelry cement and immediately place the gold end caps in place.

14. Add the jump rings to the loops on the end caps (instructions for adding jump rings are on page 21). Then add the clasp to one of the jump rings.

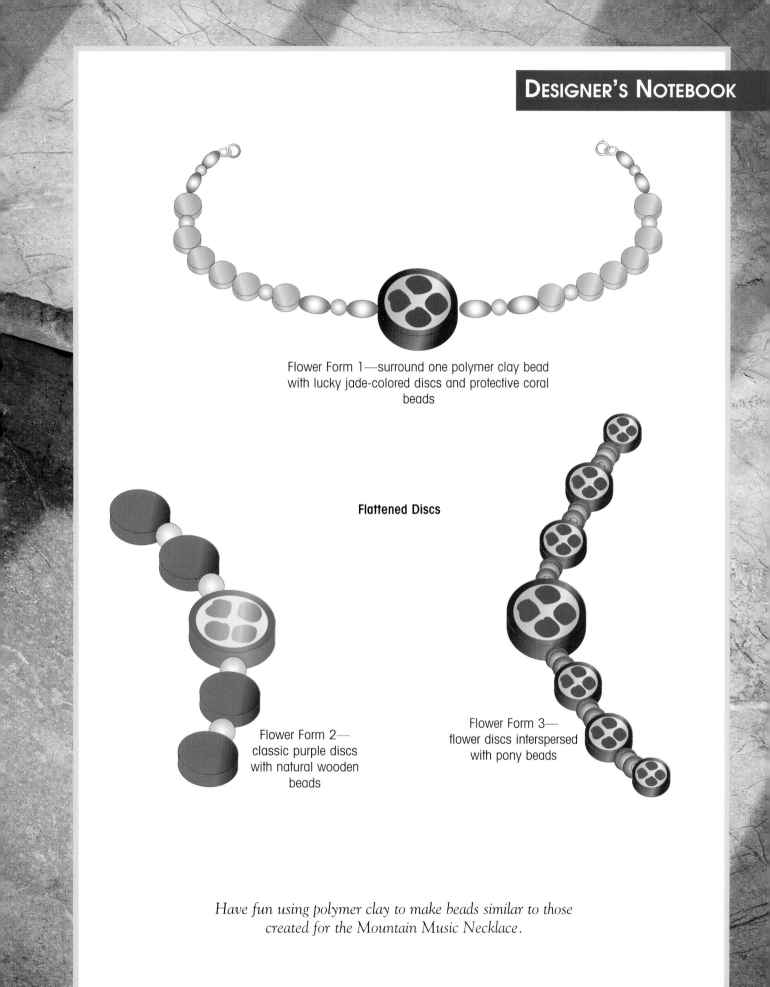

Flower Form 1—surround one polymer clay bead with lucky jade-colored discs and protective coral beads

Flattened Discs

Flower Form 2— classic purple discs with natural wooden beads

Flower Form 3— flower discs interspersed with pony beads

Have fun using polymer clay to make beads similar to those created for the Mountain Music Necklace.

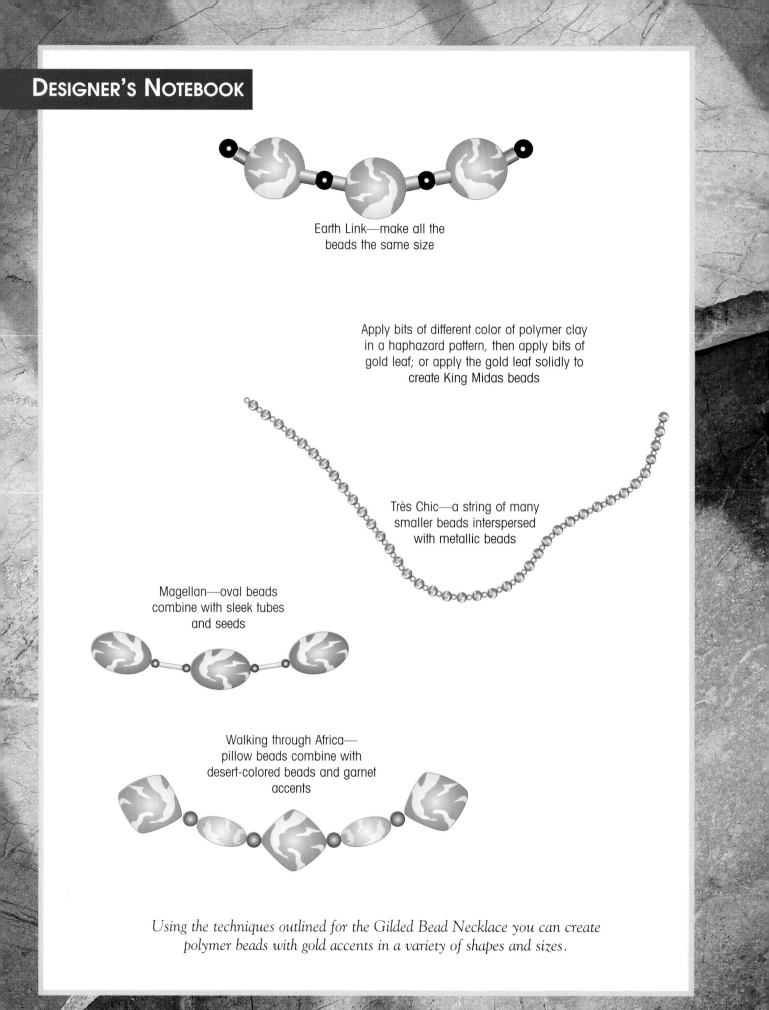

Earth Link—make all the
beads the same size

Apply bits of different color of polymer clay
in a haphazard pattern, then apply bits of
gold leaf; or apply the gold leaf solidly to
create King Midas beads

Très Chic—a string of many
smaller beads interspersed
with metallic beads

Magellan—oval beads
combine with sleek tubes
and seeds

Walking through Africa—
pillow beads combine with
desert-colored beads and garnet
accents

*Using the techniques outlined for the Gilded Bead Necklace you can create
polymer beads with gold accents in a variety of shapes and sizes.*

APPENDIXES

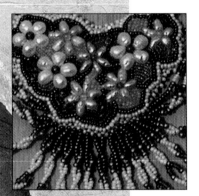

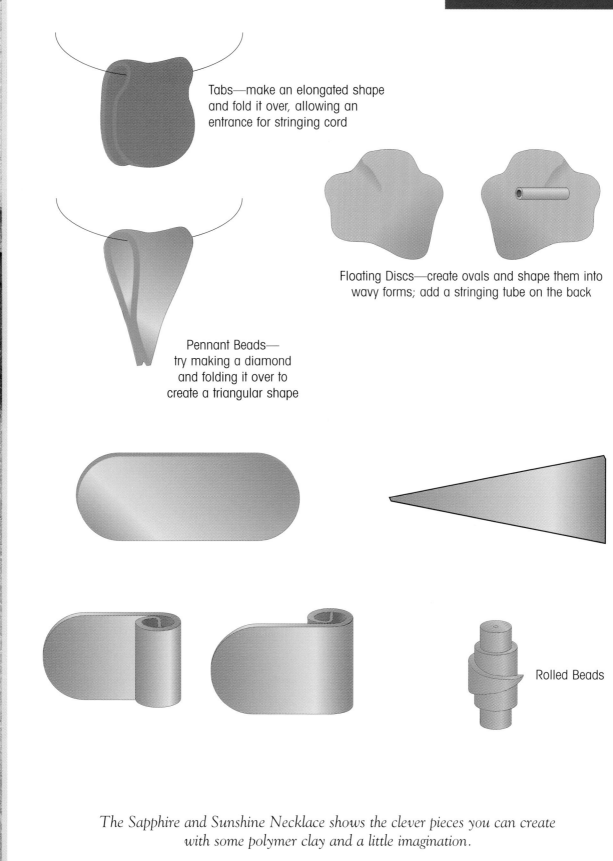

Tabs—make an elongated shape and fold it over, allowing an entrance for stringing cord

Floating Discs—create ovals and shape them into wavy forms; add a stringing tube on the back

Pennant Beads— try making a diamond and folding it over to create a triangular shape

Rolled Beads

The Sapphire and Sunshine Necklace shows the clever pieces you can create with some polymer clay and a little imagination.

BEADWORK GALLERY

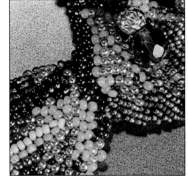

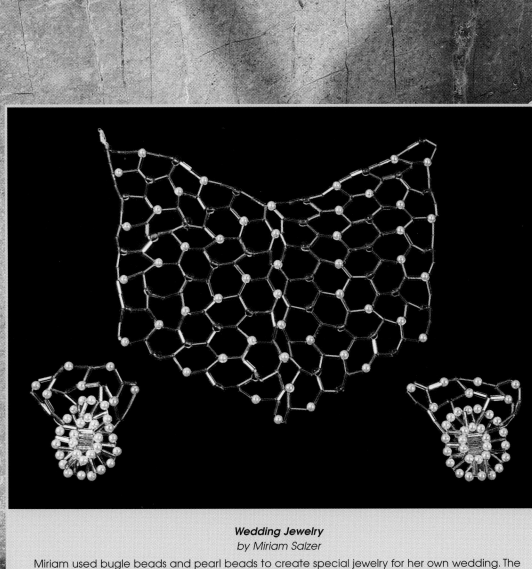

Wedding Jewelry
by Miriam Salzer

Miriam used bugle beads and pearl beads to create special jewelry for her own wedding. The large hair ornament in the center is a bun cover; beside it are matching shoe clip ornaments. Another hair ornament and a bracelet (not shown) complete this wedding ensemble.

Arizona Skies
by Catherine Lippert
Using the rosette stitch, Catherine fashioned beautiful turquoise cabochons into a brooch and matching earrings. The beads used in this piece are iris three-cuts in pale pink and green, blue iris twisted bugles, and turquoise chips.

Amulet
by Bette M. Kelley

This piece is a self-portrait made with components left over from Bette's life in the 1970s. To make this exciting piece, Bette used bugle beads, seed beads, wooden beads, mother-of-pearl fetishes, horn, a scarab, and coral from a broken bracelet from Hawaii that her mother wore in the 1940s.

Byzantium
by Bette M. Kelley

While Bette was researching the Byzantine era for a different project she was struck by the beautiful jewel tones of that time and created this necklace based on that inspiration. Bugle beads, seed beads, metal findings, and handwoven hang cords—all simple, easy-to-find materials—make up this elegant piece.

Flower Necklace
by Nome May
Inspired by her grandmother's turn-of-the-century jewelry, Nome worked antique seed beads, amethyst, garnet, and 12 karat gold-filled beads around freshwater pearls.

Red Dragon
by Nome May

Nome considers the dragon a strong guardian spirit because it is both beautiful and fierce. The fringe carries out the fiery effect she intended, and it incorporates garnets as well as glass beads.

Wandering Through Summer
by NanC Meinhardt

NanC used seed beads, glass, semiprecious beads, and floss to create this asymmetrical floral necklace using bead embroidery. This piece has nice texture and wonderful color.

Regal Collar
by Sandy Forrington
Sandy developed a technique for transposing tatting patterns into beadwork. The lace effect creates a lovely texture.

Color Splash
by Regine
What a bold piece of jewelry! Regine combined pure hues of polymer clay to achieve sharp contrast, and she fused the pieces in different arrangements to create visual interest. German Plexiglas beads and leather complete the piece.

APPENDIXES

APPENDIX A: BEAD SIZES

SEED BEADS PER INCH

Use these approximate counts of seed beads per inch to help plan your own designs.

Bead Size	Beads per Inch
11/0	20
8/0	12
5/0	7

SEED BEAD SIZES

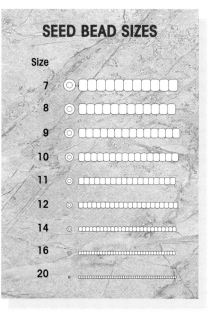

Size

7
8
9
10
11
12
14
16
20

ROUND BEAD SIZES IN MILLIMETERS

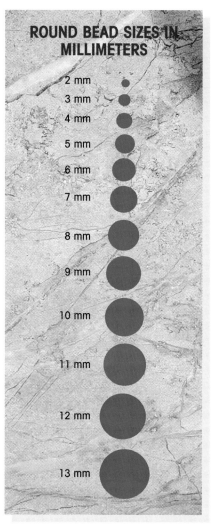

2 mm
3 mm
4 mm
5 mm
6 mm
7 mm
8 mm
9 mm
10 mm
11 mm
12 mm
13 mm

OVAL BEAD SIZES IN MILLIMETERS

Use this handy guide to measure oval beads and cabochons.

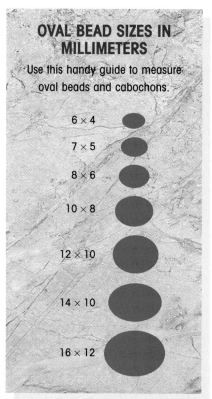

6 × 4
7 × 5
8 × 6
10 × 8
12 × 10
14 × 10
16 × 12

BUGLE BEAD SIZES

1 2 3 5

APPENDIX B: STANDARD JEWELRY LENGTHS

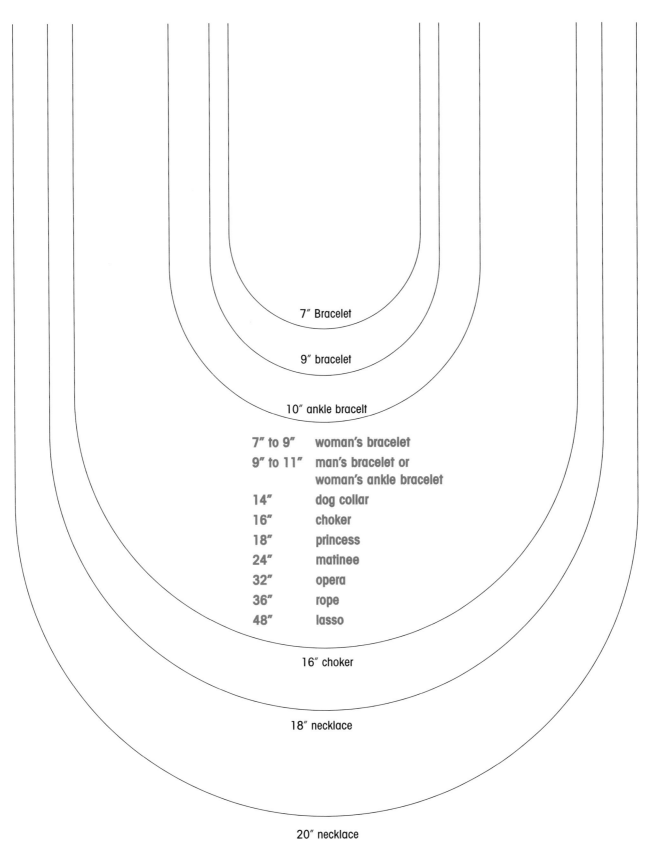

7″ Bracelet

9″ bracelet

10″ ankle bracelt

7″ to 9″	woman's bracelet
9″ to 11″	man's bracelet or woman's ankle bracelet
14″	dog collar
16″	choker
18″	princess
24″	matinee
32″	opera
36″	rope
48″	lasso

16″ choker

18″ necklace

20″ necklace

APPENDIX C: JEWELRY FINDINGS

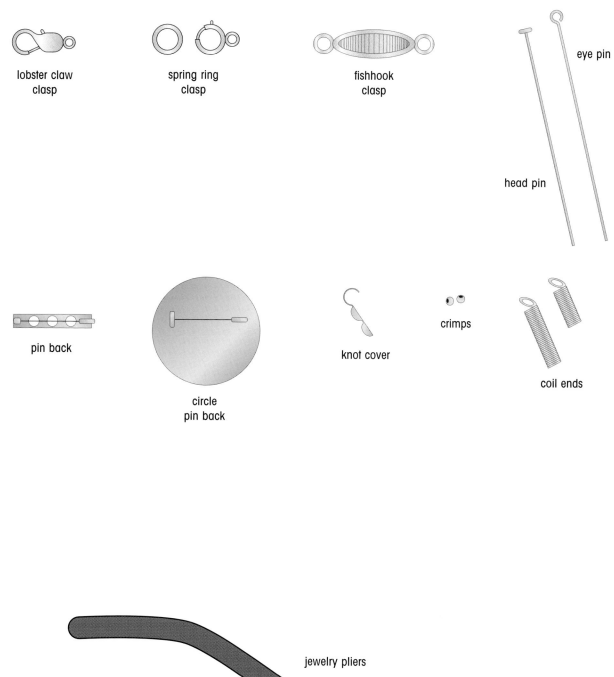

lobster claw
clasp

spring ring
clasp

fishhook
clasp

eye pin

head pin

pin back

circle
pin back

knot cover

crimps

coil ends

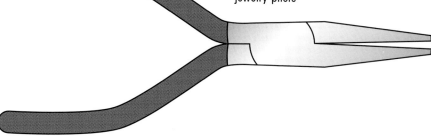

jewelry pliers

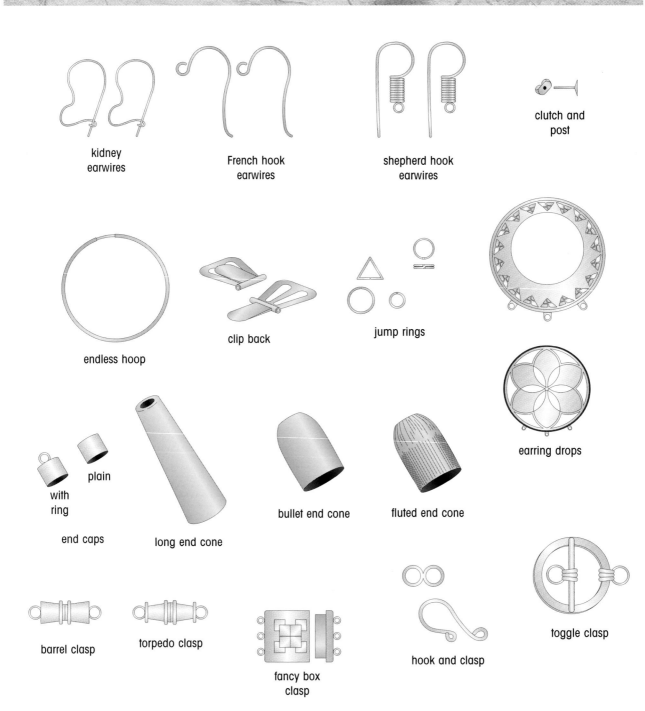

kidney
earwires

French hook
earwires

shepherd hook
earwires

clutch and
post

endless hoop

clip back

jump rings

earring drops

plain

with
ring

end caps

long end cone

bullet end cone

fluted end cone

barrel clasp

torpedo clasp

fancy box
clasp

hook and clasp

toggle clasp

APPENDIX D: PRECIOUS AND SEMIPRECIOUS STONES

PRECIOUS

DIAMOND The Queen of Gems, most desirable when nearly colorless and flawless. Also prized in canary yellow. Many less expensive grades are available for craft work. According to legend, diamonds assure a long life and joy.

EMERALD A beautiful green beryl. Expensive because it is hard to find without inclusions and cloudiness. Real emeralds are a lighter color than the name implies. Deep green emeralds are usually dyed.

RUBY A red corundum. Ruby is pink-red rather than brown-red like a garnet.

SAPPHIRE In its most familiar form, a deep blue corundum. All colors of corundum are called sapphire (for example, yellow sapphire) except red corundum, which is called ruby. Sapphire allegedly prevents poverty and death by poison.

SEMIPRECIOUS

AGATE Fancy agate comes in a variety of colors, from yellows to browns. Blue lace agate is a lovely baby blue with lacy white. Moss agate is gray with green mosslike sections throughout. Black moss agate is black and clear.

ALEXANDRITE This interesting stone appears grass green in artificial light and red in natural light.

AMAZONITE Apple green or blue-green stone.

AMBER Translucent orange-yellow resin.

AMETHYST Translucent purple stone.

AQUAMARINE Transparent blue, blue-green, or green beryl.

ARAGONITE Translucent yellow stone.

AVENTURINE Green or red-orange opaque stone.

AZURITE Azure blue opaque stone.

BLOODSTONE Green stone sprinkled with red jasper.

CARNELIAN Translucent red-orange stone.

CAT'S EYE Chrysoberyl or chalcedony featuring chatoyancy.

CHRYSOCOLLA Opaque to translucent mineral that ranges in color from sky blue to green.

CITRINE Translucent yellow stone that resembles topaz.

CORAL Opaque sea creature. Branch coral is thin like a fine tree limb, whereas stem coral is chunkier. Coral comes in yellow and white besides the ubiquitous orange-pink-red shades.

FLUORITE Purple or green translucent stone.

GARNET Transparent brownish-red (root beer) stone.

GOLDSTONE Aventurine closely spangled with (real) gold particles.

HEMATITE Shiny opaque stone sometimes called Alaskan black diamond.

HOWLITE Opaque white stone with gray swirls; often dyed other colors.

JADE (NEPHRITE) Opaque stone that is usually green; available in intense red and striking purple, too.

JASPER Opaque quartz; comes in named forms such as desert, leopard skin, Picasso, picture, poppy, rainbow, zebra, and fancy. (The names only hint at what these stones look like. Check them out at your local rock shop.)

LABRADORITE Gray-green stone with an occasional shimmer of rainbow color.

LAPIS LAZULI Opaque cobalt blue stone that is often flecked with white but is most desirable in solid blue. This stone was loved by the early Egyptians. It is often simply called lapis.

LAPIS NEVADA A pink, turquoise, and white stone.

MALACHITE Shiny deep green opaque stone streaked in black.

MOONSTONE Translucent white to bluish stone.

MORGANITE A rose-colored beryl.

ONYX Opaque black stone, often dyed a deep black; also can be dyed other colors.

PERIDOT Transparent chartreuse green stone.

QUARTZ Clear or pink stone (pink is called rose quartz).

RHODONITE Bubblegum-pink stone streaked with black.

SARDONYX An onyx having layers of (reddish-brown) sard.

SNOWFLAKE OBSIDIAN Black stone splashed with grayish-white colorings that resemble snowflakes.

SODALITE Dark blue stone striated with white. (Sometimes sodalite is confused with lapis.)

TIGEREYE Warm-brown/golden-yellow chatoyant stone.

TOURMALINE Translucent stone available in many colors; watermelon tourmaline is shaded a striking pink and green.

TOPAZ Translucent stone that is often yellow but comes in other colors, too. Blue topaz has been very popular for the last five years.

TURQUOISE Opaque blue-green stone used extensively in Native American jewelry. So-called "sleeping beauty" is unstreaked robin's egg blue.

UNAKITE Mottled green and orange stone.

APPENDIX E: BIRTHSTONES

Incorporate some of these stones into birthday gift jewelry, or simply use beads in the color of the appropriate birthstone.

TRADITIONAL

JANUARY **Garnet**

FEBRUARY **Amethyst**

MARCH **Aquamarine or bloodstone**

APRIL **Diamond**

MAY **Emerald**

JUNE **Pearl, alexandrite, or moonstone**

JULY **Ruby**

AUGUST **Sardonyx or peridot**

SEPTEMBER **Sapphire**

OCTOBER **Opal or tourmaline**

NOVEMBER **Topaz**

DECEMBER **Turquoise or lapis lazuli**

ASTROLOGICAL

ARIES (March 21–April 20) **Bloodstone, howlite, ruby, rose agate**

TAURUS (April 21–May 20) **Picasso jasper, moss agate, carnelian, clear quartz**

GEMINI (May 21–June 21) **Tourmaline, alexandrite, lapis lazuli, emerald**

CANCER (June 22–July 22) **Aquamarine, sapphire, moonstone, morganite**

LEO (July 23–August 23) **Garnet, zebra jasper, citrine, goldstone**

VIRGO (August 24–September 22) **Sardonyx, fancy jasper, peridot, poppy jasper**

LIBRA (September 23–October 22) **Amethyst, lapis Nevada, fluorite, tigereye**

SCORPIO (October 23–November 22) **Turquoise, cat's eye, obsidian, red jade**

SAGITTARIUS (November 23–December 21) **Malachite, aragonite, picture jasper, onyx**

CAPRICORN (December 22–January 20) **Blue lace agate, hematite, sodalite, azurite**

AQUARIUS (January 21–February 19) **Jade, rose quartz, amber, diamond**

PISCES (February 20–March 20) **Labradorite, blue topaz, coral, opal**

APPENDIX F: DESIGN CHARTS

General Design Graph—you may photocopy for personal use.

Brick Stitch Graph—you may photocopy for personal use.

Peyote Stitch Graph—you may photocopy for personal use.

APPENDIX G: METRIC CONVERSION CHART

The following list will help you convert measurements given in this book from inches to centimeters (or millimeters) and vice versa. Measurements greater than ½ inch are rounded to the nearest .5 centimeter. One inch is equal to 2.54 centimeters exactly, and 1 centimeter is equal to .3937 inch.

⅛″	= 3mm	13″	= 33cm
¼″	= 6mm	14″	= 35.5cm
⅜″	= 1cm	15″	= 38cm
½″	= 1.3cm	16″	= 40.5cm
⅝″	= 1.5cm	17″	= 43
¾″	= 2cm	18″	= 45.5
1″	= 2.5cm	19″	= 48.5
1¼″	= 3cm	20″	= 51
1½″	= 4cm	21″	= 53.5
2″	= 5cm	22″	= 56
2½″	= 6.5cm	23″	= 58.5
3″	= 7.5cm	24″	= 61
3½″	= 9cm	25″	= 63.5
4″	= 10cm	26″	= 66
4½″	= 11.5cm	27″	= 68.5
5″	= 12.5cm	28″	= 71
5½″	= 14cm	29″	= 73.5
6″	= 15cm	30″	= 76
7″	= 18cm	31″	= 78.5
8″	= 20.5cm	32″	= 81.5
9″	= 23cm	33″	= 84
10″	= 25.5cm	34″	= 86.5
11″	= 28cm	35″	= 89
12″	= 30.5cm	36″	= 91.5

Beader's Glossary

ABALONE Iridescent pieces of shell (mother-of-pearl); also called paui (or paua) when blue-green in color

AMULET An object that is worn to bring supernatural protection to the wearer

ART DECO Decorative art style expressed by strong linear lines and shapes; popular from 1915 to 1940

ART MODERNE Style from the 1950s characterized by kidney shapes, geometrics, and chrome

ART NOUVEAU Style characterized by soft flowing lines and foliate forms; popularized by Alphonse Mucha, Aubrey Beardsley, and others from 1890 to 1915

ARTS AND CRAFTS MOVEMENT Reaction to the onslaught of industrial production; a return to handcraftsmanship

AURORA BOREALIS Beads with an iridescent finish (literally means "northern lights")

BANGLE Endless circle bracelet

BAROQUE Irregular-shaped bead that is lumpy rather than smooth (for example, freshwater pearls); also an art style from the seventeenth and eighteenth centuries characterized by elaborate ornamentation

BEESWAX Bee product used to strengthen thread, prevent unwanted tangles, and enable easier threading

BEZEL Strip of metal or other material used to set cabochon stones

BICONE Bead with a wide center and narrow ends

BOHEMIA GLASS Beads made in Czechoslovakia by displaced Venetian glass artists

BOLO TIE Leather thong slide that is a popular accessory for Southwestern attire

BONE Hand-carved beads made from animal bones; some mimic ivory

BOTTLE GLASS African beads made of recycled green and brown glass

BUGLE Tube-style bead

CABOCHON Gemstone or paste stone with a smooth, rounded top and a flat back; usually set with a bezel

CALOTTE Metal crimp used to end a strand of beads

CANEWORK Glassmaking technique in which colored rods are used to create complex patterns; also used as a technique for creating polymer clay beads

CAP END Metal cap-shaped finding used to finish an end

CEYLON Pearlized finish for beads

CHATOYANT Certain stones with a changeable luster or color and a narrow band of light (like cat's eye and tigereye)

CHIPS Small, irregular-shaped precious or semiprecious stones

CLASP Jewelry closure usually made of metal

CLOISONNÉ Finish technique in which bright-colored enamels are separated by metal channels and baked to create beautiful beads and other objects.

CRIMP Tiny metal ring used to secure ends of jewelry

CRYSTAL Leaded glass beads, usually faceted; also a blanket term for any clear glass bead

DANGLE Any item suspended from an ear wire or other jewelry finding

DICHROIC GLASS Prismatic glass made of layered oxides

DOG COLLAR Very close-fitting necklace (about 14" long)

DONUT BEAD A large flattened disc with a large hole

dZI Agate bead from the Himalayas that is decorated with stripes or, most preferred, eyes

EAR CUFF Small half-crescent of metal worn on the ear; may be plain or have dangles

EAR DROPS A metal ornament (fancy or plain) from which dangles are suspended

EARRING Any ornamental jewelry worn on the ear

EBONY Black wood used for beads; may be carved or smooth

ETHNIC BEADS Primitive beads of many different materials and designs; usually come from Third World countries

EYE PIN Long wire with a loop at the end

FACETED BEADS Beads with cut surfaces that refract light, creating rainbows

FETISH A primitive charm

FILIGREE Ornate, open-weave pattern, often found on metal clasps

FIRE POLISH Glass exposed to extremely high heat to create a special finish

FOCAL POINT The large centerpiece of a piece of jewelry

FOLK ART Naive designs with a homey flavor

GALVANIZED Coated with zinc

GOLD FOIL Actual gold rolled extremely thin; sold in booklets of "leaves"

HAIR PIPES Long, ivory-colored bicone beads used in Native American jewelry

HEAD PIN Flat-headed length of wire

IMPRESSIONISM Art style with an emphasis on capturing the color of light

IRIDESCENT Used to describe a bead that looks as if it were dipped in oil to create a special finish

IRIS BEADS Beads with a special rainbow coloring

JAPANESE SEED BEADS Large-holed seed beads

JUMP RING A circle of wire used to attach two jewelry findings or to finish off a string of beads

KNOT COVER Metal clamshell-shaped finisher used to hide knots; also called a bead tip

LAMPWORK BEADS Handwrought glass beads made using a lamp

LANTERN BEAD Cylinder-shaped bead faceted with gold detail

LINED BEAD A bead that is coated inside with another color, often a metallic

LINSIN Disc-shaped bead with a hole running from side to side through the center

LUSTER BEADS High-gloss beads

MILLEFIORI Glass or polymer clay beads with very ornate patterning resembling bouquets of flowers (literally, "1,000 flowers")

MOKUME Unique circular patterning found in glass and polymer clay beads

MOTHER-OF-PEARL Beads or pendants of carved shell, as from abalone; also called nacre

NIOBIUM Metal heated to a high temperature to produce permanent iridescent coloring (magenta, turquoise, etc.); used for findings

OPALESCENT Reminiscent of the coloring of opals

OPAQUE Solid-colored beads that do not allow the transmission of light

POINTILLISM Art style concerned with color effects (for example, using yellow and blue beads that the viewer's eye will mix to create the perception of green)

PONY BEAD Large-holed bead

POP ART Art movement in which common objects and commercial imagery were used (the classic example is Andy Warhol's art depicting soup cans)

RATTAIL Soft, satiny cord used for jewelry

ROCAILLE Seed bead with a silver lining

RONDEL Flattened, donut-shaped bead

SATIN Bead finish reminiscent of satin cloth

SCARAB Beetle-shaped bead of Egyptian origin; signifies long life and rebirth

SPACER Bar with holes used to keep different strands of beads separated; also a term for less important, secondary beads used to build up a beading design

SPLIT RING Double circle of wire used as a jewelry attachment; alternative to the jump ring

STABILIZED BEADS Powdered gemstones (especially turquoise and opal) mixed with resin to create beads

STRIATED BEADS Beads with marblelike streaks of color

SURREALISM Art movement in which dream images are used in abstract, amorphous ways

TAIWAN SEED BEADS Beads of quality similar to the Czech seeds but usually available at a lower cost

TALISMAN An object that is worn to bring good fortune

THREE-CUTS Seed beads with faceted sides and ends

TIGER TAIL Nylon-covered steel wire used for bead stringing

TRADE BEADS Beads actually used for trade; the term encompasses many types of beads but generally refers to African beads

TRANSLUCENT Smoky; such beads allow some light to enter but are not clear

TRANSPARENT See-through, clear

TRIBAL BEADS Beads of specific tribes or, commonly, beads of primitive design

TUBE Bugle bead

TWO-CUTS Seed beads with the sides faceted

VICTORIAN Decorative style named after Queen Victoria characterized by heavily ornamented, romantic designs, often with motifs of angels, flowers, and ribbons

Recommended Reading

Bagley, Peter, *Making Modern Jewellery*, Cassell, London, 1992.

Benson, Ann, *Beadweaving*, Sterling/Chapelle, New York, 1993.

Bevlin, Marjorie, *Design Through Discovery*, Holt, Rhinehart, and Winston, New York, 1963.

Birren, Faber, *Ostwald: The Color Primer*, Van Nostrand Reinhold Company, New York, 1969.

DeLange, Deon, *Techniques of Beaded Earrings*, Eagle's View Publishing, Ogden, Utah, 1983.

Fitch, Janet, *The Art & Craft of Jewelry*, Grove Press, New York, 1992.

Henzel, Sylvia S., *Collectible Costume Jewelry*, Chilton, Radnor, Pennsylvania, 1987.

Kenzle, Linda Fry, *Dazzle: Creating Artistic Jewelry & Distinctive Accessories*, Chilton, Radnor, Pennsylvania, 1995.

Kenzle, Linda Fry, *Embellishments*, Chilton, Radnor, Pennsylvania, 1993.

Kidd, Alexandra, *Beautiful Beads*, Chilton, Radnor, Pennsylvania, 1994.

Kunz, George Frederick, *The Curious Lore of Precious Stones*, Dover, New York, 1971.

McConnell, Sophie, *Metropolitan Jewelry*, Bulfinch Press, Boston, 1991.

McCreight, Tim, *The Complete Metalsmith*, Davis Publications, Worcester, Massachusetts, 1991.

Miller, Harrice Simons, *Costume Jewelry*, Avon Books, New York, 1994.

Moss, Kathlyn, and Alice Scherer, *The New Beadwork*, Abrams, New York, 1992.

Nassau, Kurt, *The Physics and Chemistry of Color*, John Wiley & Sons, Chicago, 1986.

Pearl, Richard M., *Successful Mineral Collecting and Prospecting*, Bonanza Books, New York, 1961.

Peck, Judith, *Sculpture as Experience*, Chilton, Radnor, Pennsylvania, 1989.

Roche, Nan, *The New Clay*, Flower Valley Press, Rockville, Maryland, 1991.

Sommer, Elyse, *Contemporary Costume Jewelry*, Crown, New York, 1974.

Spears, Therese, *Contemporary Loomed Beadwork*, Promenade, Boulder, Colorado, 1987.

Stessin, Nicolette, *Beaded Amulet Purses*, Beadworld Publishing, Seattle, Washington, 1994.

Tomalin, Stephany, *Beads!*, David & Charles, London, 1988.

White, Mary, *How To Do Beadwork*, Dover, New York, 1972.

Resource Guide

SUPPLIERS

Please visit your local bead shop. Also try some of the mail-order sources listed here. Some of the following companies offer free catalogs, while others charge anywhere from $1 to $20. Since the prices fluctuate, send a postcard first.

Aardvark Territorial Enterprises
P.O. Box 2449
Livermore, CA 94550

Beada Beada
4262 North Woodward
Royal Oak, MI 48073

Bead Art
60 North Court Street
Athens, OH 45701

Bead Boppers
1224 Meridan East
Puyallup, WA 98373

Beadbox
10135 East Via Linda
Suite 116
Scottsdale, AZ 85258

BeadZip
2316 Sarah Lane
Falls Church, VA 22043

Fire Mountain Gems
28195 Redwood Hwy.
Cave Junction, OR 97523

General Bead
317 National Blvd
National City, CA 91950

Grey Owl's Indian Craft
   Supplies
P.O. Box 340468
Jamaica, NY 11434

International Beadtrader
3435 S. Broadway
Englewood, CO 80110

June Tailor, Inc.
P.O. Box 208
Richfield, WI 53706

Kuma
Box 2712
Glenville, NY 12325

Ornamental Resources, Inc.
P.O. Box 3010
Idaho Springs, CO 80454

Personal FX
P.O. Box 664
Moss Beach, CA 94038

Polyform Products, Inc.
P.O. Box 2119
Schiller Park, IL 60176

Shipwreck Beads
2727 Westmoor Court SW
Olympia, WA 98502

Sunshine Discount Crafts
P.O. Box 301
Largo, FL 34649

TSI, Inc.
101 Nickerson St.
Seattle, WA 98502

PERIODICALS

Adornments
P.O. Box 177
Fox River Grove, IL 60021
   Linda's new bead and wearable art quarterly. $20 per year.

Bead & Button
Conterie Press, Inc.
316 Occidental Ave. South
Burke Building, Suite 316
Seattle, WA 98104

Bimonthly magazine in color. Covers handmade jewelry and buttons.

Lapidary Journal
Devon Office Center, Suite 201
60 Chestnut Ave.
Devon, PA 19333-1312
   Carries regular feature on beaded jewelry and a must-have "Bead Annual."

Ornament
Ornament, Inc.
1230 Keystone Way
Vista, CA 92083
   Beautiful full-color quarterly focusing on artistic jewelry and art-to-wear clothing.

NATIONAL AND INTERNATIONAL BEAD SOCIETIES

Almost every state has one or more bead societies. Check at your local bead store for location.

Bead Study Trust
Mrs. Hugh Brock
12 Richmond Road
Oxford OX1 2JJ England

Center for Bead Research
4 Essex Street
Lake Placid, NY 12946

Center for the Study of Beadwork
P.O. Box 13719
Portland, OR 97213

Society of Bead Researchers
1600 Liverpool Court
Ottawa, Canada K1A 0H3

The Bead Museum
140 S. Montezuma
Prescott, AZ 86303

Index

About the Author

Portrait of a Woman after *Lucas Cranach the Younger*
by Linda Fry Kenzle

Linda Fry Kenzle, well-known artist and designer, is the author of many books, including *Embellishments* (Chilton, 1993) and *Dazzle: Creating Artistic Jewelry & Distinctive Accessories* (Chilton, 1995). Linda's award-winning work has been shown both nationally and internationally and is in collections in the United States, Europe, and Australia. She teaches and lectures on color, design, technique, and creativity.

For lecture and workshop information write to:

Linda Fry Kenzle
P.O. Box 177
Fox River Grove, IL 60021

email:
http://www.lkenzle@concentric.net

1/8"	= 3mm	13"	= 33cm
1/4"	= 6mm	14"	= 35.5cm
3/8"	= 1cm	15"	= 38cm
1/2"	= 1.3cm	16"	= 40.5cm
5/8"	= 1.5cm	17"	= 43
3/4"	= 2cm	18"	= 45.5
1"	= 2.5cm	19"	= 48.5
1 1/4"	= 3cm	20"	= 51
1 1/2"	= 4cm	21"	= 53.5
2"	= 5cm	22"	= 56
2 1/2"	= 6.5cm	23"	= 58.5
3"	= 7.5cm	24"	= 61
3 1/2"	= 9cm	25"	= 63.5
4"	= 10cm	26"	= 66
4 1/2"	= 11.5cm	27"	= 68.5
5"	= 12.5cm	28"	= 71
5 1/2"	= 14cm	29"	= 73.5
6"	= 15cm	30"	= 76
7"	= 18cm	31"	= 78.5
8"	= 20.5cm	32"	= 81.5
9"	= 23cm	33"	= 84
10"	= 25.5cm	34"	= 86.5
11"	= 28cm	35"	= 89
12"	= 30.5cm	36"	= 91.5